THE ANATOMY OF A BEST SELLER

3 STEPS TO DECONSTRUCT WINNING BOOKS AND TEACH YOURSELF CRAFT

SACHA BLACK

CONTENTS

For Cassie... You know what you did, you naughty minx.

RULES AND SHIT

Reading is one of the closest things to magic. And if you disagree... well, you're just plain wrong. It's a precious thing. We're taught as children, in the arms of parents and loved ones, to open our minds, fill our brains with wonder and worlds. When we read, we visit newfound places and worlds ladened with colors we don't have and creatures that shouldn't exist. Our brains draw rich images from wood pulp and ink, our hearts shudder with emotions for people that don't exist. What part of that isn't sorcery?

Now, readers, well, they experience magic. That's one kinda drug. I'm partial to it, I won't lie. But writers... we're the makers and creators of this mystical crack. We are the original magicians, pulling not rabbits but worlds from empty hats. And isn't that some kind of magnificent?

I like to start each craft book with a short spurt of necessary hyperbole. See, I don't like books that work in "must-dos," "have-to-dos" and "always". Fuck that. *Rebel*, my sweets. Rebel till your heart turns dark and your stories weep with the blood of your enemies.

That said, this book is going to contain some techniques

and while I might say "you need to do this or that," I don't mean it prescriptively. You don't have to do shit. I'm not your book-mama, I don't dish out spankings... well, actually... Umm, never mind, wrong kind of textbook.

Look, the point is, don't let anyone tell you there's only one way to do something. I don't believe there's only one way to learn, and that's the case for craft too. I'll tell you what there is only one of though... *you*. Only one author with your specific lens, your specific voice, and your specific way of looking at the world and characters. So, if you don't like the craft-noodles I'm serving, you can get a different take out. I'm not precious.

Actually, that's a lie. I'm wildly precious. I never intended to write this book, but now I have, I'm giddy with excitement to share it. The techniques folded between these pages are just the things I do. I didn't realize others saw them as useful and would want to use them too. But then... aren't all the best books surprises?

What I'm trying to say is that everyone likes to dish out rules. I'll probably do it in here. But rules were made for breaking. You do you, Boo.

What This Book Is About

This book is about writing. Actually, it's about reading. Maybe it's about learning. It's about best sellers. Scrap that. It's about all the above.

If you want to improve your writing and be the best writer you can be, then at some point you're going to have to be active and do something about it. You're going to have to learn. Some people take courses, some people listen to podcasts or watch YouTube channels, others read craft books. All of those options are valid. I personally dabble in a bit of everything. I probably always will. That is the fate of the perpetual learner. But see, there's another kind of learning that I think is possibly the most powerful of all.

Self-learning.

Except that us sensitive writers like to poison our brains and riddle our minds with doubt and a lack of confidence. Surely we can't just teach ourselves? We don't know what we don't know.

Bitch, please.

Did I not start this very chapter discussing the absolute magnificence that is our ability to conjure magical absurdities from fuck-nothing save the gooey biologically gray carcass inside our skull?

I did. Don't look back, it was rhetorical.

People... *We are fucking magicians.*

YOU... You are a magician. You might not know things right now.

But you can discover them.

You can be Indiana Jones and Howard Carter. If archeologists can dig up dinosaur-mummy bones, you can be damn sure us lowly writers can unearth a technique or two all by our onesies.

I know it's scary to... to trust oneself. But it's going to be okay. I've got your back.

This book will show you how to read differently. It's going to make you stop, then take a hot second to figure out the recipe for reader-crack.

If you're yet to find a method to teach yourself craft, this one might help. Try it, see if you're Cinders and the glass shoe fits.

I should warn, this book might change the way you read. But if it does, that doesn't mean you can *only* read this way forevermore. Let's not all be extremists, shall we? There's too many of them in the world as it is. You want to read for pleasure, go do that. You want to read for pleasure the first time and then do the analysis? Cooooool, I'm not here to stop you.

Some Caveats

- **You're not interested in developing your craft.** I mean... do we really need to cover this? If you're happy with where your writing is at, this book probably isn't for you.
- **You don't want, or aren't willing, to try reading in a new way.**

Pulls face

Henry Ford said, *"If you always do what you've always done, you'll always get what you've always got."* There is one exception to that. If you like the way you read, and you feel you're getting enough techniques and tools from them because you learn by osmosis, then outstanding. You're one of the lucky ones that doesn't need to intentionally dig deeper. That's okay, read the book for info and take everything with a pinch of salt.

But if you want to get more from the books you're consuming, if you want to deepen your craft, then let's mix it up. We're going to put some razzle with your dazzle, try the unicorn pen, and sprinkle glitter in your ink. It's go time, bitches... which brings me to my final caveat...

- **You don't like dark humor or swear words.**

It's a well-known fact I've never been what "society" deems a lady. If you don't like it, ciao baby, it's been real.

Still with me?

Excellent.

Let's get reading.

WHAT IS A BEST SELLER ANYWAY?

Is it just me or have you ever had a moment where reading has felt more like riding a shroom high as you dance in la-la land, and tripped off your tits at the exquisiteness of a book world?

No?

Just me?

Anyone?

Jeez, hard crowd.

Alright, but I bet you have totally and utterly fallen in love with a story at some point. You must have or you wouldn't be reading this—a book about how to actually, you know, *do* that to other readers.

What is a Best Seller?

It seems pertinent to actually define what I mean by a "best seller" before we get too far into the book. Why? Because what you might think of as a "best seller" at face value is not quite what I'm going for here. Let's think of "best seller" as a tub of Neapolitan ice cream. For those that don't know, that's a tub of ice cream which has a strip of vanilla, chocolate, and straw-berry. Basically, the stuff of a '90s baby's dreams.

You got your bog-standard vanilla flavor of best seller like the New York Times (NYT) list. Vanilla is the most common flavor for a reason. It's bland and palatable to most people. Which is why the NYT is vanilla in the ice cream tub because that's the type of best seller most of us think of when someone says, "best seller". Included in this are the USA Today, Sunday Times, Wall Street Journal or any of several other lists touted as accolades by the "names" in the industry.

And yes, those are best sellers in the most recognized sense. But those lists are owned by traditional publishing and often doused with a heavy dose of curation over data. So even if you outsold the vast majority of books on the list, it doesn't actually guarantee you a slot on the list.

Ugh. Where's the spice, people? Give me a bit of strawberry, or even chocolate with chili in it.

Which leads me to other types of best seller. Let's go with chocolate ice cream next. There are Amazon best sellers, both those in the overall top 100 of all books sold on the site and then smaller Amazon category best sellers. These elicit digital, high pitched, hand flaps of excitement because you get a little orange tag by your book's title. And of course, there are similar chart toppers on Kobo or Apple or any of the other stores you sell your book in.

And last, we have strawberry with sprinkles and butter-scotch sauce and whipped cream. The most unique type of best seller.

This one is determined by you.

Maybe there's a book that to your knowledge hasn't ever hit a "list". But it was translated to film and then the sales picked up and it sells consistently and you just love the characters and the prose and you wish you were as good as that author.

Or maybe there's a book in an obscure niche that doesn't sell mind-boggling numbers but sells consistently. You're okay with that because if you had ten books in the niche, you'd earn enough to quit your day job. It wouldn't make you seven figures, but you don't care because the world building is to die for and you cry with laughter every time you read the genre.

Or maybe there's a book no one's heard of and doesn't sell well, but it's simply exquisite. You see yourself in the characters and it's meaningful and deep and you like the theme and the narrative voice and you wish you could write like that.

These examples, under my definition of "best seller" in this book, count. I'm using "best seller" as a catch-all term. Would I do that in general conversation or if I were teaching marketing? No. Of course not. But that's not what we're doing here. In this book, we're focusing on anatomy and a process for digging up tools you can use. Where those tools come from is almost irrelevant. What's relevant is your goal. What you want to achieve, what you want to write like, how and what you want to improve. I want to help you uncover the tools and techniques your favorite authors use. The authors who inspire you or make you green with envy. The books that made you sob and laugh, the ones that fifteen years later you're still thinking about. Whether or not they got an orange flag on the seventy-sixth of whenever is irrelevant. I want to know what you deem as good, as best, and amazing.

That's what's important here.

Your opinion.

Perhaps we need to be clear on what our definitions of success are? Because you can be a best seller and earn six or seven figures without being Stieg Larsson. Am I saying you shouldn't strive for Fifty Shades of success?

OMG NO.

I'm not afraid to say I'd love that level of success. Hell, it's what gets me out of bed and keeps me motivated every day. But I'm also aware that if I don't focus on what's in my control, what's in my ability to influence, then I'll lose my tiny fucking mind, shit the bed, and watch as my success swims happily downstream. All I, all any of us, can do is control how well we set ourselves up for potential success.

What is your goal?

To be on the NYT list? Then yes, you should probably focus on deconstructing books that have actually been on the list. If you want to be a screenwriter, then applying these tools to movies and shows is more important than applying it to books. Whatever your goal, there's space for you here, too.

If it's not the NYT you're after, then I wouldn't bother looking at the hardback NYT list for deconstruction. That's going to be full of John Grisham, Nora Roberts and James Patterson. Remember, the list is owned and dominated by traditional (trad) publishers and there's an element of "editorial choice" that goes into the final list, not just sales. That doesn't mean you can't find best sellers in the indie community or on other lists, though. You only have to look at the number of six and seven-figure indies to know that.

It doesn't matter if you want to be the top selling author New York has ever seen, or if you want to be the niche queen of romantic alien frog erotica. What matters is you're aligning your definition of "best seller" to the choices you make for deconstruction.

Do you want to be a trad published author? Then you should deconstruct the highest selling traditionally published books in your genre.

If you want to be an indie player in an indie dominated genre, then deconstruct the best of the best in that genre.

After that, if you decide what you've found in the books you've deconstructed doesn't meet your expectations and desire for writing, then it's a different conversation. It's one about goal alignment and pivoting. Either you change the type of story you want to write to meet the requirements of the genre and readers, or you don't. But remember that risks not giving readers what they want. Last, you can pivot genres and find something that makes you happier.

All options are valid. The question is whether you're happy with the consequences of your choice.

Ultimately, you can write whatever story you want. You have permission to just write for yourself and to get out the story you have to tell. But you can't then expect the market to gobble it up. Not unless it meets their requirements as well—but unless you've done the research and know the market, chances are it won't meet reader requirements as well as it could—we'll cover this later.

It's always about choice, about choosing this path or the other.

Right now, all you have to do is align your deconstruction with your goal.

You want big NYT status, make sure you're deconstructing big NYT books. You want big indie success? Deconstruct big best-selling indie books.

The skills and tools I'll be showing you in the book are applicable to any kind of best seller, any kind of story, movie, TV show, Broadway musical (or other type of medium) that you deem of quality. Character development is character development. Plot is plot.

Know your goal. Know your path and, brick by brick, build your potential.

The Anatomy of a Best Seller

So why the title?

This book is far more practical than anything else I've written. But let's get one thing completely clear before we get into deconstruction... Can I—or any other craft wielding nonfiction geek—give you the cut and dry formula to this-is-how-you-bake-and-sell-a-mind-blowing-blockbusting-book?

No.

Really, truly, fucking Earth-core deep, *no*.

Of course not.

There is no secret recipe that can guarantee success. There is only setting yourself up for success. This will not be the last time I talk about potential success. It's the thing I wish new writers understood. This game, this book industry... it's really about iteration and trial and error. It's about attempting to give the market what it wants, and the slow and laborious method of, reader by individual reader, cultivating an audience.

This creates the potential for success.

Iterate enough times, successfully give the market what it wants, and you give yourself the best chance of success.

But it doesn't guarantee it.

Some people think lightning bolts happen when you do something right. That you work just the right way and life, the universe, and the magical dolphin of Zeitgeist will come along and sprinkle a cheeky glitter-gasm of success on your book and it flourishes.

It doesn't work like that.

I'm more of a setting-up-for-potential-success-enough-times-I-beat-the-odds girl.

When most people think of "best seller" they think of Stieg Larsson, whose books went viral posthumously, or E. L. James, Stephenie Meyer, Suzanne Collins, or, She Who Must Not Be Named. But these authors had more than just best seller status. They were the lightning bolt to end all lightning bolts. Too often we mistake "best seller" for that unpredictable roller-coaster of impossible circumstances that arise and have a slice of WTF-just-happened attached. You can't predict that. Only prepare for it.

What we can do, though, is examine what is already successful (to you) and break it down. If you see a beautiful mansion and you want to build a house like it, what do you do? You speak to the builders to find out what bricks were used, how much concrete was needed and how deep the foundations went. You talk to an architect and study the schematics and drawings, the skeleton of the building. I'm betting you'd break down what the builders did, so you can use similar tools to build a house of your own. But maybe you change the color of the bricks, add a conservatory on, and a loft conversion. It doesn't come out quite the same, instead it comes out bigger and better.

That's what we're going to do here.

We're going to peel apart the covers of your favorite books, the authors you'd like to emulate, and deconstruct what they've done. We're going to dig into the anatomy of those books like a brain surgeon and forensically slice the tools out so we can use them ourselves.

On Reading this Bad Boy

As this book is so practical, I want you to work while you read. There are intermissions where I give you tasks to do while reading the following section. That's because while this book contains facts and information, it's heavily based on a process. A process that only works if it's implemented. So when you come to an intermission and it tells you to do something...

Pretty please, with a cherry spanking on top, do it.

This book focuses on three ordered steps:

1. Read
2. Deconstruct

3. Implement

Surprising no one, that is the structure of the book too, and it's the order in which we will progress.

Ready?

Excellent... here's your first task...

INTERMISSION

We interrupt your reading of this book to bring you a task. This book and topic are a little different. More task based than anything I've written before—workbooks aside, of course. But I want you to do the work alongside the reading.

So, your first task is thrice:

- Find or purchase a pencil. Or if you're aghast at the prospect of marking a book, dig up an e-reader.
- Purchase a butt-load (and yes, that's a measurement) of sticky tabs.
- Choose—purchase or borrow from the library*—a book from your favorite author, an author you admire, someone you'd like to be as good as, or whose voice you deeply appreciate.

If you're a rereader of books, then I'd recommend picking a book you've read many times as it's easier to be objective about and less caught up in the story. If you're not a rereader, just plump for a book that fits the above.

. . .

*Don't mark your library books though, prepare for copying out the sentences you like.

That's it for now. We'll begin reading soon.

STEP 1 READ

1.0 READ

Where we fill our eyeballs with glitter crack, discuss the fact Stephen King is wrong, ponder our fragile little egos, trip off our tits, and consider why we should all bash more coconuts.

The Fear of Reading Like a Writer

I think people are resistant to reading like a writer for two reasons:

1. They fear it will detract from their love of reading.
2. It skirts a little too close to comparison.

First up, I get it. You've read for escapism since you came flailing out yo mama's special place. It brings you joy and respite from daily drudgery. Most of us are in love with reading. We fall for characters and worlds; we covet the way characters make us feel things. Often cited as the most common hobby or leisure activity globally, reading is popular. Who wants to lose their favorite pastime?

But let me reassure you, this isn't a prescriptive method, and it's not a one-way road. You can take a return journey if you don't like it.

Point two, it skirts too close to comparison. Sigh. I know, I know. For some, the famous quote 'comparison is the thief of joy' is real. I understand the fear that in deconstructing someone's work, you're essentially looking at it to examine the differences between your words and theirs. But I believe there are two ways to look at comparison: fear-based comparison and constructive comparison.

Fear-Based Comparison

Fear-based comparison, also known as comparisonitis, is the compulsion to compare your accomplishments, skills, or work to another's in order to determine its significance or relative importance. This results in negativity, doubt, and a raft of other deliciously parasitic mind worms. There are some people who find the perceived "gap" between where they are and where they want to be generative. In that it drives them to act to shrink the gap.

For those for whom it causes pain, there's a way to look at comparison differently to help prevent the formation of this poisonous mindset. Especially if any kind of comparison is unhealthy and bad for your headspace. I understand we're all different and that's okay. If this has been you, then I'm going to challenge you to look at this method, anyway. If it doesn't work, let's cross that bridge later.

Constructive Comparison

I'm one of those people who fall into the "comparison is

positive" group. I think that's why I came to this type of learning so quickly. Don't freak out, but I want to be honest. Constructive comparison is at the heart of this book. It's comparing, but for a purpose, for learning, and for figuring out the mechanics behind success.

Essentially, when reading and deconstructing I look at an author's work *not* to establish who is better or worse. But merely to examine the differences and similarities between their work and mine.

That's it.

I don't assign emotion to those differences or similarities. I take them on face value. They give me information. I ask myself whether I'm happy with what I've discovered. Do I like the tools this author has used? If so, can I use them too? Or maybe I can put my own spin on them.

It's a learning exercise. It's an opinion forming task. It is an assessment of tools and strategy and a decision-making process that follows.

Doesn't seem too bad after all, hey?

Why You Need to Read Like a Writer

There are famous quotes that tell you to read. That it's essential. Hell, most of them claim you can't possibly be a writer unless you read. The problem with such quotes as these is they're vague and entirely unhelpful.

"If you don't have time to read, you don't have the time (or the tools) to write. Simple as that." Stephen King.

> "Read, read, read. Read everything—trash, classics, good and bad, and see how they do it. Just like a carpenter who works as an apprentice and studies the master. Read! You'll absorb it. Then write. If it's good, you'll find out. If it's not, throw it out of the window." William Faulkner.

Yes, yes, oh wise and worldly word-gurus, but WTF does reading lots or reading like a writer even mean?

We're getting there. Stick with me for a bit longer.

There's something magical about reading a text, stopping when it shakes your bones and hits you in the feels. But it's even more amazing when you stop and analyze the work and finally figure out how the writer did it.

See, in deconstructing, you'll learn not only that you like something, but why you like it and how the crafty bugger of an author did it, too. And isn't that an amazing feeling? As a writing-reader, when you can narrow your eyes into a glint, let a smug grin peel across your lips because...

You know...

You seeeeee the author...

And you *knooooow*...

It's like the sky opens and rains down epiphany on you, as your eyeballs fill with glitter and author-crack. Once you realize *how* an author did something, you have the power and tools to do it too.... But in your own way.

What's interesting to me is our ability to read develops far faster than our ability to write. Arguably, when we come to write our first book, many of us have read hundreds or even thousands of books. We already have ten thousand hours of reading under our belt. And yet, the first draft of our first book is usually comparable to a giant mold-covered turd. It needs burning in a sacrificial rite of passage and never spoken of again.

So why, when we've read all our lives, can't we write how we want to? Because we've spent our lives reading like a reader, not reading like a writer.

That's what we're going to rectify.

1.1 TWO TYPES OF READING

"Some books are to be tasted, others to be swallowed, and some few to be chewed and digested; that is, some books are to be read only in parts; others to be read, but not curiously; and some few are to be read wholly, and with diligence and attention." — Francis Bacon, *The Essays*

The What, Why and How of Reading

The vast majority of "regular" readers—the fans we're looking for—read at a surface level. Let me be clear and say, there's nothing wrong with that, especially if you are a reader and have no interest in writing books.

But, if you have lofty ambitions to hit the best seller lists, if you want a red-carpet runway on your book's premier movie night, if you want adoring swathes of readers lavishing you with fan art and gift boxes, then you're going to have to read a little differently, at least occasionally. And that is at the heart of this book. Before we can deconstruct, our reading habits need to become more observational.

Reading like a *reader* will help you develop your writing technique, but reading like a *writer* will inject steroids into that process and jump jack you up the craft stream to "boss level 5000" (according to my eight-year-old this is a legitimate game level boss, so let's run with it).

As a "reader" when you read, it's usually unconscious, and thus forms a shallower level of reading. Your brain loses itself in the plot and therefore you only get the "what" of the story. You take in what's going on—the plot—but nothing else. You experience, engage with, and understand it.

But as a writer, you want to get to an enhanced type of reading. When you start to ask "why" the author created the story, characters, and words, you simultaneously take a step deeper into understanding but outward from the plot to become an observer. The holy grail is to go deeper still and understand the "how" behind their authorial choices too. That's where you want to be as a writer. Digging into the author's psyche and analyzing their technical choices.

Okay, I'm sure there are arguably many types of reading. But for the sake of this book, we're going to agree there are just two types that we care about:

- Reading like a reader
- Reading like a writer

Let's dive into a little more depth on these.

Reading Like a Reader

Everyone starts with this method of reading. It's what we're taught in school, and as toddlers, what our parents aim to teach us.

To progress to the next type of reading, we must master this type first. This reading is what 99 percent of the population does. They achieve the gold standard of reading like a reader and then they stop.

Readers appreciate and understand the "what" of what happens in the story. That's it.

- Boy is chosen.
- Boy goes on a quest and finds a magical device of power.
- Finally, boy slays the dragon.

This is plot and it's our first and most shallow encounter with any story. This kind of reading is pleasurable. When I truly lose myself in a book, it's the "what I'm reading I'm engaging with." I don't read with my eyeballs. My mind opens up, the words disappear and I watch the characters as if it were regular TV. I guess that's why there are so many quotes about readers living a thousand lives. I want to be clear that even though I'm advocating for a different type of reading, I still fundamentally believe this kind of reading is and always will be essential as a writer.

Why?

Because reading for pleasure is pleasurable and we can all do with a little more pleasure in our lives... Ahem.

Pleasure also tells you things...

If you can stay even a little aware while diving into escapism and you can recognize when you're deep in a story, or when you're being punched in the feels by an author, or when they made you ugly cry, that teaches you about story. Even without stopping to analyze every inch of the line that made your eyeballs sweat, your subconscious will notice things; methods and tools the author used. You'll get a sense of the shape of a story, how it flows and peaks and troughs from chapter to chapter. This is valuable. You need this.

This feeds your ability as a writer to know story shape innately.

Don't stop yourself reading for pleasure. We need to do both types of reading. Escapism, joy, allowing our subconscious to swallow us in story, and the analysis and deconstruction as writers.

Reading like a reader, means you understand the "what" of what is happening. You connect with characters. Love them. Like them. Even loathe some of them. But you don't venture deeper than that. Readers hold hands with books, they dance around the maypole and sing and laugh and feel things together. Writers, when they truly read as a writer, well now, they do something completely different.

The Why of Reading

Then we go to school. English teachers get very concerned with the theme and meaning behind stories. See, they think we writers are profoundly deep and are constantly trying to weave important philosophical meanings into our story.

Side eye

What they don't appreciate is half the time we've written these stories with our thumbs up our asses, minds in reverse, brains deprived of caffeine and are simply "making shit up". And actually, this is a good point. Most authors don't realize, or don't consciously, pump their stories full of golden tools or literary devices. They're just writing intuitively, from the gut, vomiting words onto the page. But that is what happens when you've learned craft and internalized story and prose. Do you drive your car consciously? Didn't think so.

But, for the sake of our fragile egos, I'm going to pretend that we are always as diligent and intentional as our English teachers suggest.

Suffice to say, school teaches us to dig a little deeper than the surface level plot. We clutch the story duvet and slip our sticky mitts beneath to see what's there. We understand the why. The meaning of the story and the purpose.

We figure out the why by either digesting and pondering the story ourselves or talking about it with friends or teachers.

Reading Like a Writer: The How of Reading

Reading like a writer is wildly different. I like to think of it as closer to demonic possession than hand holding and maypole dancing.

Reading like a writer means becoming a student, *reading* like a student. Instead of lying back and passively taking it... it, being the story... obviously...

Erm...

Instead of passively absorbing the story, you engage with it on a deeper level in order to understand the mechanics that made it work, that made it a best seller.

I want you to split reading into two: experiences and observations. Take this first line from *Trey*, the third book in my YA fantasy series:

"The darkness is violent."

Reader experience: ooh, something has gone down. What the hell is going to happen next?

Writer observation: In the first sentence, the author has used personification. Darkness cannot be violent, it is only the absence of light, therefore the author has given it a humanlike quality to create imagery. I've seen a lot of personification of the weather, but less the light and dark, so this sticks out as a tool I could use in the future. And because it's the opening line in the finale of a trilogy, it's likely foreshadowing, an omen of the trouble about to come in this book. Opening lines are often tools used to influence the rest of the plot, like foreshadowing.

You see the difference? Observing can then lead to the discovery of tools or devices or ideas that you can use in your own writing, like personifying the light. But you'd use the tool in a different way or different context in your own work.

This is where the magic really happens because to understand how a writer creates the story they've written, we need to reverse engineer it. Deconstruct the tools they've used. Take it apart brick by brick in order to piece the findings back together in our own work. This is reading like a writer.

It's being a student. A reading-architect. A book chef.

It's reading a book, and diving into its construction. Reading like a writer means you understand the mechanisms the author used to create the story and impact.

These levels of reading aren't separate. More like layers. They build and build, one on top of the other as you step further and further into the book.

Show and Tell

When I was at university, some of my course pals used to take the piss. I'd get half an hour into the lecture and then nod like a dog. I'd passed out for a couple of minutes, and then snap wide awake again. Poor lecturer. It really wasn't their fault. I'm just not good at being lectured. I don't want to be told anything. But unfortunately, this has been the prevalent model of teaching for... well, forever. Teach' stands at the front, points at the board and pretty presentation, and tells us stuff we need to remember.

But there's another way. What about scientists, researchers, archaeologists? They learn by discovery. Sleeves rolled up, fingers dug into the grimy sludge of soil, books, and experiments. These guys figure stuff out as they go.

I've always been more inclined to this style of learning. I'm a "give it here and let me try" learner. And I honestly reckon a lot of us are. When we "discover" for ourselves, rather than being told, it's enlightenment. It's an ecstasy driven braingasm waiting to happen.

Is there anything better than that "ah-ha" moment when you figure something out all on your own? I don't know about you, but I feel smug as fuck when that happens. And you should too. We did good, people. When we "discover" of our own accord, we *understand it* more intimately, more deeply and more profoundly than when we are told. We've engaged with the information or revelation by investigating and reflecting on it. And of course, for the teachers now twitching while reading this, I'm aware methods have progressed to encourage this kind of learning too—don't throw the book away just yet.

The problem is, so many of us lack confidence in the things we know or discover. We don't believe our findings are valid because an expert didn't tell us. Never is this truer than in deconstructing fiction. It is not always the physical written words we need to analyze in a story. Often, it is what is not said that gives us the most truth.

Unlike nonfiction, where truth must be concisely and clinically laid bare on the page, fiction is a different beast altogether. Truth lingers with ghosts in the shadows between the lines. How can anyone tell us what ghosts whisper when everyone's ghost is a little different?

There is no expert, only you, darling.

Sometimes we have to learn by doing, by throwing our virginal rumps into the fray and praying the bum-bruises don't hurt too bad. This type of learning is just as valid as your boss queen lecturer explaining the moral ambiguity of Shake-spearian characters.

Your thoughts, your discoveries, and learnings are all valid. Super fucking valid. Everything we know to be true today was discovered by someone who didn't know it before. Don't under-sell your capability. Have faith in yourself.

Besides, not to get too scary too early... but there's no teacher here. No one to ask when you deconstruct. Just you and the book, and much as we might want it...

The book doesn't answer back.

One More Time for the Road

Last time I'm going to say this. No one's saying you have to *always* read consciously. Nor am I saying you have to read a whole book like that.

Reading like this has a purpose. You only need to decon-struct when you want specific information or learning. If you want to read for pure escapism, do it. Don't make reading a chore. Besides, with a bit of practice, you can have your book-cake and eat it. You can retain your joy of unconscious escapism, dance into consciousness to observe something fancy, and go back to la-la land again. I don't think anyone has said it better than Francis Bacon, *"Some books are to be tasted, others to be swallowed, and some few to be chewed and digested"* and isn't that what we're saying here? You have the flexibility to decide whether you're going to swallow the thing whole Scooby Doo style, or take delicate bites like the lady I am...

If you can't stand the thought of this type of reading, cool, don't do it. Keep your permanent unconscious escapism read-ing, and instead, try rereading. The first read of any story is usually an immersive experience. But once you've read the story, you can't un-read it or un-know it. So you're naturally a little more conscious than you were the first time round. Just like watching a movie, the first time you're usually utterly engrossed, but the second time, you can make a cup of tea and you won't have lost the thread of the action. And like movies, the second time you read, you're able to pick up the subtle clues and foreshadowing you missed the first time.

1.2 HOW MUCH DO I HAVE TO READ?

Oh, honey, I ain'tcha word mama. You get to determine how much you read. No one is going to tell you how many books you *should* or *have* to read. I'm not sure 'how much' is even the right question. Do you feel you're reading enough? Yes. Then you're reading enough.

We all have different input requirements. I need to consume a lot of books in order to have enough creative inspiration to write. More specifically, I need to read IN the genre I'm writing in. But some people need to read other genres than the one they're penning war and peace in. We're all different. Is there something specific you want to learn or improve? Then it's probably time to crack open a book or thrice.

If you think you could watch one less episode of *Gossip Girl* a week in favor of an additional hour of reading, also good. If you sit and watch four hours of TV every night (and be honest now, sweetie), then chances are, you could probably cut that down by one of those hours a night in favor of reading.

But do you have to?

Hell no.

You do you.

Whatever your situation, no one is judging.

That said, if you want to class yourself as a writer, then you have to do at least *some* reading, and in my humblest of opinions, that means effective reading. Run with logic if nothing else:

Would you pay an architect who didn't study buildings to design your house?

No?

Of course not. At least, I wouldn't be paying some mofo unless he was deeply passionate about rivets and divots, beams and planks, glass thickness, brick density, and material styles. If I'm having a house designed, I want my architect to be the geekiest motherfucker alive. That bitch better eat, sleep, and shit bricks, or I'm out.

And thus, shouldn't we be the same over our words? I suspect our readers want us to tell the best story we can. And the only way to do that is to roll up our proverbial sleeves and figure out some story stuff.

I'm not here to tell you *what* a good story is. I'm going to show you how to figure out what *you* think a good story looks like. Ultimately, while 'story' has some commonalities, each genre is their own unique shade of monster. They all have nuances and niches, quirks, and oddities. So, woe betide I try to do that for the thousands of niches out there.

No. Better to equip you with the tools to break down your genre and favorite stories so you can give your readers exactly what they want.

And that, really, is the point of this subsection. Deconstructing best sellers will increase your vocabulary, improve your craft, give you new literary tools and devices to sprinkle into your work and it will help you work out what's at the heart of your genre so you can deliver the best book possible.

Sacha, Give Me Some Fucking Numbers

Alright, Jesus, pushy today, aren't we?

First, I have a question for you. How much data do you need to make a decision? Cause that's how many books you need to read.

And there's a point here too.

What's your goal?

If your goal is to pick up tools and devices from a book, then there's a deep-dive analytical deconstruction where you pummel drive your way through just one book to scour it for all its literary goodness. Then there's the more comparative type of reading suited to understanding and knowing a genre. For comparative reading, you need a wider spread of data to gather conclusions on patterns and, you need to read more than one book because one book does not a genre make.

So, I say again, what's the goal?

grins

Whaddya trying to achieve?

Some writers will be comfortable making a decision on little data, others will need hoards of the shit before they can come to a conclusion. There's no right or wrong answer here. You need to read enough books to feel comfortable. If your goal is genre knowledge and you can read three to five books and be confident you can deliver the same, but better, that's your answer.

For me, specifically, I can draw conclusions after as little as two or three books if I notice fundamental similarities that influence the plot on a structural level, or if I know the elements are common to the genre. In my mind, two is a connection, three is a pattern.

When approaching a new genre, if I want to "write to reader" (also phrased, write for the reader), then I'll consume books. As I wrote the first draft of this book, I'd read twenty-three books in the new genre I'm approaching. As I'm editing this, I'm now on the thirtieth book. At twenty-three books read, I didn't feel confident enough to write in the genre. But reflecting now as I'm editing and adding this line, at book thirty, there's been a shift. I finally feel like I'm ready to write. That said, I suspect I'll double that figure in the next six months before I feel like I know the genre inside and out. But that's my personal needs. Am I suggesting everyone should read that many?

Fuck no.

I have no life, so I read a LOT. I lean towards reading more in a genre than not because I'm riddled with doubt and anxiety. The book-data massages my lack of confidence. I over-read to find facts, trends, and patterns that are replicated multiple times. Then I can be certain of what I do and don't need to include in my books.

But that absolutely does not mean you need to do the same.

There is another point here too. Reading loads doesn't mean you're reading deeply or wisely. If you're skimming 666 books a year, it's unlikely you're getting the depth you need from those books to know your market or take any tools from the best-selling authors. Likewise, if you've only read one book in your genre, even if you've read deeply and comprehensively, you've probably not taken in enough inspiration, tools and lessons to create your own voice or understand what the market wants.

All I want is for you to feel confident you've nailed down the important trends and patterns in a genre. Confident enough to know your reader and understand what they want.

Okay... with that in mind...

Your number is...

However many books it takes for you to feel certain you know what you need to know.

That was a dick move, wasn't it?

Toothy grin

Soz.

Mmkay, go figure out your number and then you have permission to abuse your bank with book purrrrchases.

1.3 MIMICRY

"Most of us find our own voices only after we've sounded like a lot of other people."—Neil Gaiman, Masterclass.

Mimicry has a bad rap. But evolutionarily speaking, mimicry is, in part, responsible for our development. Monkeys learn to use tools by mimicking and copying their elders. Sure, originally, via happy accident, a monkey will have figured out that bashing a coconut against a tree will split it. But then the younger generations copy and mimic the use of the tool. But even though they copied, they won't all use the tree in the same way. Some throw the coconut. Other monkeys hold the coconut against the tree and bash a rock on it. Then there are the monkeys who smash the coconut with both their hands against the tree and don't forget those that only use just one hand to whack the coconut.

Whatever they do, the result is the same: they get to drink the sweet milk inside.

Babies learn to crawl and then walk by copying their parents.

When you teach a baby to talk, you sound out the words

over and over for them until finally they sound the word correctly.

So why is writing any different?

Am I saying you should directly lift Neil Gaiman's words from his books and plant them in your own work?

Sweet mother of literary universes, no.

That would be plagiarism and copyright infringement.

In no way am I suggesting you directly lift an author's words and put them into your own work. That will lead to a swift cancellation on social media, a potential lawsuit, and a boatload of embarrassment. So let's chuck that thought in the fuck-it bucket and move on.

Am I saying you should deconstruct Gaiman's work to find out the tools he used and then use those tools in your own work?

Yes.

Imitation *is* iteration.

But, but, but...

No, seriously, imitation is iteration.

But how can that be?

Okay, real talk. Neither you, nor I, nor any smart-ass writer can be Neil Gaiman. The only person who can accurately write, like Gaiman, is Gaiman. Take art forgers. You know the reason they're called forgers? Because they usually get caught and while they might get close to replicating a masterpiece like for like, experts can always tell the difference. We are all unique individuals with unique histories and experiences that shape our worldview. The moment you apply a device or tool from one sentence to another, you're iterating it. And if you're not, then you're plagiarizing it by copying it like for like.

Imitation is iteration.

Frank Sinatra and Michael Bublé. Bublé is often compared to Sinatra because they share similarities in tone, and type of songs. Sinatra has clearly been an influence on Bublé, but they're not the same. Everyone can tell the difference between them because they sound different.

Remember the monkey?

You should be like the monkey.

While one monkey originated the coconut-rock bashing, each monkey found its own way of interacting with the rock-tool. That's what you need to do. Take the tool and make it your own.

Now, that said, sometimes, for some brains, handwriting out another author's sentence to learn what it feels like in your hand, to write with the same flow and pace, can be useful. But that is wildly different to cutting and pasting another author's sentence straight into your actual book file. Don't do that. Only dicks do that, and you're not a dick, are you?

ARE YOU?

Good.

"This is about helping your voice grow in its technical quality. For those of you who are worried you're going to 'sound' too much like someone else, you're not. This is about breaking down an author's prose in order to learn what technical aspects of craft they use. This is not about taking a quote from an author and using a thesaurus to replace the words so you're writing in their style. This is about understanding the possibilities of prose. It's about understanding the methods and techniques you can use to flex sentences and create description and dialogue or punctuation, etc. Then implementing those new methods and tactics into your own work."
Sacha Black, *The Anatomy of Prose.*

Right, now everyone has calmed their tits about copying. Let's look at the ways in which we can mimic.

Example of Mimicry

I picked up the last book I finished, *A Lesson in Vengeance* by Victoria Lee, and I opened to a randomly tabbed page. This was the quote I underlined:

"It's guilt reaching long fingers into the soft underbelly of my mind and letting the guts spill out."

So first, let's look at what Lee does in this sentence. What tools is she using?

In a bout of telling, she identifies the emotion the character is feeling: guilt. But then, she flips the tell on its head and personifies the emotion by giving it limbs and making those limbs "do" something. They act and have agency. Let's use those tools and "mimic" without copying.

It's fear; legs of steel crawl under my ribs and kick the ivory cage until my lungs splinter and my breath runs dry.

I used the exact technique she did. I named an emotion. Then I described it by personifying it with limbs, and giving it agency through action. Here, though, I tried to mimic the sensation fear creates. The visceral panic and rapid breathing.

Let's do another example. I picked out *The Hating Game* by Sally Thorne. She uses a punctuation trick to heighten the heart-pounding intensity of sex scenes, like so:

"He demonstrates. Throat. Breast. Ribs. Hips."

The technique here is more obvious. One-word sentences that create a staccato word-beat-word-beat rhythm feel. In this instance, it creates the gasping intimacy of lovers. But we could take that same technique and apply it to say... fear.

"I freeze. Blink. Inhale. Scream. Run."

You can mimic without copying. You can use the tools and devices other authors use without plagiarizing.

This action of mimicry is at the heart of the implementation.

But more on that later.

Mimicry Methods

All mimicry was not created equal.

There's a lot in each sentence. There are words for one. The overarching meaning, there could be individual devices like metaphors, punctuation, the rhythm, and flow. When a lot of authors come to reading like a writer and using devices and tools they pick up, there's often a mistaken perception they have to mimic the entire sentence. But mimicking all of it in one go is hard.

You don't have to. You can slice and dice like your everyday serial killer and just grab aspects or elements of a sentence to mimic.

For example, we take the last sentence we used from Ms. Thorne, and instead of naming body parts, we name physical actions. But we could just as easily have used it with character names, or description of an object or person. Perhaps we could have taken the essence of rapid punctuation and done it with two-word phrases. Or maybe it inspires you to create a repeating pattern. Perhaps you write a sentence of description, then a series of one-word sentences followed by description, and then a repeat string of one-word sentences etc. Mimicry isn't always about using the tool like for like, take it out of context, use it in new ways.

Bend. Shape. Create. Iterate...

Did I just...?

1.4 A METHOD FOR CHOOSING WHAT TO READ

In the introduction I asked you what your goal was because your goal should lead your reading when deconstructing. But what does that really look like? Let's grab a scalpel and play surgeon. It's time to get stabby and slice under the skin of our goals.

Know Thyshelf... Self?

The first part of this journey is always the most painful. You need to know yourself. Can you blindly study authors and learn stuff? Yes, of course. But if you want to improve your writing, it makes much more sense to be tactical in your choices about what to learn. Where are your skills and where are your weaknesses now? What genre are you writing in? What feedback have you had previously that's showed an area for improvement?

When you decide to take an expensive course, you don't just randomly dive into any old course and hit buy. No, you've thought it through, you've saved up your pennies for the one course you really want.

Don't embark on studying an author unless you know what you're after. What do you want to achieve or improve? What's your goal here? Yes, you could wade in rudderless and just "pick shit up", but you can also drive a boat into the Atlantic without a compass, radar, or location software too. Wonder how that would go for you.

I get that there are a ridiculous number of books in the world. There are literally millions. So how in Satan's name do you know what to choose, read, and dissect? I'm here to help, or perhaps give you a methodology for choosing.

Non-Comparison Authors (comparison, henceforth shall be known as "comp")

There are a couple of schools of thought on reading outside your genre. Some people are ardent followers of the read wide arena. Others refuse and stick to their lane. I'm indifferent. Do as you please. For me, I like to pick up tricks and tips from all kinds of authors. I think you can pull tricks and devices from a range of places. Just because it's a horror technique, doesn't mean you should avoid all things creepy in fantasy. Perhaps it will heighten the atmosphere. Maybe it will raise the tension. But this brings me to the next interconnected point.

Books that simply appeal to you. It is a constant surprise to me that the general reading population doesn't read as widely as most authors I know do. It's a lesson I have to learn and relearn. My friend reminded me of this the other day. He's a whale reader, reads two to five (plus) books a week—all of them science fiction dappled with the occasional fantasy. That's it. Doesn't read anything else. It's an enigma to me. But anyhoo. As authors, we tend to have a wider reading base than the average reader. So if a book from a different genre calls to you, there's probably a reason. Dig into it, deconstruct the book, understand why you like it and what tools were used to create the effects that drew you in.

Learning Specificity

Then we come to what I think is the second most useful choice—second only to comparison authors, which are so important they have their own section. If I have something specific I want to learn, then I hunt out books reported to be good at that thing. Let's say you're writing a fantasy book, but you have a subplot where your protagonist is dealing with grief. Well, reading books that deal predominantly with grief and dissecting what they do, the tools they use, and how they cover grief will help. The grief author is creating the same emotional feels that you're after in your subplot. The fact they're in a different genre is irrelevant because you can take the tools and emotions they're using effectively to create the firework emotions you're after in your own story.

While I write Young Adult, I can pick up skills for improving suspense and tension from reading thrillers. I can pick up methods for making my romantic plot lines more swoon-worthy if I read more romance—any best-selling romance. I can create richer descriptions if I read epic fantasy. And so on.

To find relevant books, I'll ask friends for recommendations. I'll throw a question out on Facebook or social media. A simple post asking for recommendations for a specific thing always garners responses. After all, there's nothing readers enjoy more than sharing their love of books.

Seminal Works in Your Field

I've never been much of a fan of classics, but early work in a niche can sometimes help to give you a grounding and understanding of what's at the heart of a genre.

Last, we have comparison authors, but that requires an entirely new section...

1.5 COMPARABLY COMPARED: AUTHORS AND BOOKS

A comparison author is an author who writes in the same genre AND sub niche as you. Their books have similar themes, tropes, or settings. For example, *The Hunger Games* and *Divergent* series by Suzanne Collins and Veronica Roth, respectively, are both Young Adult dystopian series. If you like one, the chances are, you'll like the other. Thus, they are comparison authors.

If you like James Patterson's thrillers, you'll probably like John Grisham or Tom Clancy—they're comparison authors. Have you ever heard someone say oh, it's Harry Potter meets Percy Jackson? That's a comparable author pitch. If you know and understand who and what Harry Potter and Percy Jackson are, then you'll probably love whatever story it is the author is pitching.

This kind of conversation often leads to a serious clenching of the buttocks because who wants to compare themselves to George RR or Stephen King?

Listen, it's going to be okay. Loads of writers get this wrong. They think they should look for authors with a similar voice or authors at their same level of success.

Nope, and nope.

It might surprise you, but this isn't even about you as the author. It's about the reader. Think about the last time you rolled into a bookstore or library and struck up a conversation with the book seller. You probably said something like "Yo, I like James Patterson and John Grisham, who else d'ya recommend?" The bookseller then uses Patterson and Grisham to trot off and find you other books you'd like. The new books you get handed...? They're comp authors for the authors you first suggested.

Why choose comparison authors to deconstruct? Well, if you want to succeed in a genre, then understanding what the popular authors are doing helps. Popular authors are already feeding a hungry audience with exactly what they want—hence their popularity. So it makes sense that you should figure out what they're succeeding at and do that... only better.

Cackles

This is the heart of writing to market. First you find a hot category, then you do the work of figuring out what the bestselling authors are doing, and proceed to rinse and repeat.

The only way to know who your comparison authors are is through research and reading. Okay, so how in literary hell's name do we find comp authors?

What You Need to Know

First up, you need to know some information about your own book. Does your book have to be written?

No.

Do you need to know all of this information?

Again, no.

But knowing some, or in an ideal world, all of it will help you narrow down the selection of potential comps. Do you have to match all of these items in your comparison books? Nooooo. That would result in finding, like, one book... *yours*!

- The overarching genre *(e.g., fantasy)*
- A more niche category or subgenre *(e.g., steampunk fantasy)*
- Similar books that inspired you to write
- Your theme
- Other books you've seen that you think are in the same genre
- Books with covers similar to what you want *(as long as those covers are found in your genre and they're not covers you like from other random genres)*
- Any tropes you may have used
- Heroine's journey / heroes journey
- Your tone *(dark, lighthearted, humorous, parody, political)*

How to Find Comp Authors

First, let's just address the gremlin in the room. A lot of writers struggle with finding comp authors. They see a pretty cover and decide that's a comp author or decide to read that. But I want to push on the analysis aspect. It's one thing for a book to look like it's in the correct subgenre but, like, have you ever picked up a book based solely on the cover, read it and felt... cheated?

Mm-hmm, and this is exactly why you got to do both parts of this work. Making the book package—cover and blurb—look and feel good, ain't enough. That might get you an initial sale, but it won't get you a returning customer.

E-book Categories

On your book's (or any book's page) will be a section labeled "Product details" or "publisher information" or something along those lines. Don your specs and head for the categories section. This will be whatever the author has chosen in the metadata section when uploading their book. For example, "Teen & Young Adult Fantasy Romance eBooks" "Political Thrillers" "Satire Fiction".

Click one of the categories and you'll go to a list of the top 100 books in that category. Now, depending on which store you're looking in, how curated that store is, and how marketing-savvy the author was when picking categories, you'll either have a fairly accurate list of genre books or a bit of a cluster fucked mishmash.

There's a judgment call required here. Don't trust on face value that a book from that top 100 list is definitely what you're looking for.

I look at the reviews and skim the keywords, searching for anything I might be using in my own books, like "forbidden love" or "pacey plot" or "queer romance". Then I read the "look inside" and skim the opening pages. This is usually sufficient to know whether it's similar enough to my book to be classed as a comp.

Oh, don't forget to assess the front cover. Does it look like it belongs in your genre? If so, that's a good sign it could go on your short list of books.

The "Also Bought" Section

The "Also Bought" section has waxed and waned in popularity with the Amazon store in particular. They took them away for a while. I can't keep up with if they're in use. But essentially, an also bought is a book that a reader purchased before or after buying your book. Remember the librarian above who went and got you new books based on the authors you gave them?

Same thing, only digital.

The problem here is that we indies like to splurge on marketing adventures and things like Bookbub Featured deals can skew the "Also Bought" section into the realms of royally fudged.

At the time of writing, 'Zon is calling the section "books you may like" on the U.K. store, and "explore similar books" on the U.S. store. You're looking for any section of recommendations that isn't sponsored—because this means someone is paying to place their book in this spot.

There are multiple sections that are reserved for advertising and they'll be in sections like "products related to this item" with a "sponsored" label somewhere around that area. The reason you don't necessarily want to pay attention to the sponsored books is because while the author may have targeted correctly, a reader has not purchased the book. And that's the important bit. We're trying to please readers, so we want to know the books they've actually decided to buy, not the ones they're being targeted with.

Other Suggestions

Once you find a book by an author, if the store has an author page, that's another good place to check. Take Amazon, for example. Beneath the author's profile picture and bio, you'll find a section that says, "similar authors". It's worth checking the list and hopping to the other author profiles. There you'll find a list of their books and some of them should be in the same genre. The only caveat to this is when you have an author like me, who's using the same pen name for multiple genres. In my case, you get a mix of nonfiction authors and young adult authors, which isn't helpful for anyone, me included.

Instagram is currently the love—and bane—of my life. It sucks so much money from me because I follow several "bookstagrammers" in my genre. A bookstagrammer is someone whose account focuses on promoting, sharing, reviewing and taking photos of books. Most will focus on a single genre or type of book. Which is why it's such a great place for picking up recommendations.

Other options include following or researching book bloggers, Goodreads lists, book lists, websites that focus on book recommendations or book listings. Podcasts that focus on one genre, for example, the *Big Gay Fiction* podcast run by the ineffably amazing Jeff Adams and Will Knauss, focuses on LGBT+ fiction. Or the *Fated Mates* podcast run by Sarah Maclean and Jen Prokop, focuses on romance fiction.

There are hundreds of ways of unearthing books in your genre. You just have to scratch your noggin and dig a bit.

While I have an appreciation for spreadsheets, I swear my party trick is breaking them by just looking at them. Regardless, they're super handy for creating lists of comp authors and books. I built one recently for my new genre and it has a couple of hundred books on it. Which, if you like advertising, doubles as a list of keywords for that type of advertising.

1.6 READING FOR GENRE

We're always told to read our genre. To know it intimately. To fondle it, grope it, and squeeze its plump little titties like we're thirteen and it's the first time we've ever seen a pair of baps.

What no one ever explains is why. Why the hell can't we just dive into writing? We have a story. We know what's going to happen. So why can't we just throw ourselves at the blank page and hope for the best?

Why do we have to spend eons of our precious time reading in the genre we're writing in?

Because, honey, expectations.

Look, I don't like the weight of a judgmental little munchkin any more than you do. But *'judge,'* readers will do, and if your goal is to make enough money, you can bathe in it, burn it, or wipe your butt with it, then the expectations mean something.

With any of this deconstruction stuff, you're always looking for the pattern, the connection, or the repetition.

But first, what is genre?

Defining Genre

Genre indicates a certain 'style', a grouping. A selection of characteristics found in a group of books that denote a particular style. "Characteristics" being elements like tone, content, settings, level of steam, etc.

The problem is, there's no genre police. Now the rebellious among us will appreciate the lack of genre police. But this creates an irksome task for those approaching a new genre who would prefer some rules.

There are, of course, some hardline, black and white definitions of genres—these exist at the core of a genre. Like romance must have an HEA (Happily Ever After). But when you move outward toward the limit of a genre, the lines and boundaries blend with the genres close by. For example, fantasy and steampunk. Or thrillers and psychological thrillers. When this happens, they share common threads while other threads remain distinct. For example, thrillers and psychological thrillers will both share fast, edge of your seat, pacing. They'll likely both have a darker tone and there will be twists and turns and questions and something that needs solving. Where they differ is in the setting and content. Thrillers can be global, include agents, missions, and big crimes. Psychological thrillers are often based in domestic settings. There's a house with a family, the mystery is close to home, and the perpetrator is usually someone the protagonist knows.

Right genre rules. I am not an expert in all genres, therefore I can't tell you what the expectations are for each genre. But you can use some common sense here. How do you know what to focus on when studying genre? Well, what attracted you to that genre in the first place? What is it at the heart of that genre?

Take horror, there's going to be monsters, seen or unseen, there's going to be a focus on fear and scary things, right? So that's probably a good place to start deconstructing the best sellers for "horror" genre information. How did the author describe the monster or create the illusion of a monster? How did the author elevate the sense of fear? When did your sphincter tighten? That's a good place to stop and examine what just happened.

What about dystopian stories? Well, the heart of those is a new society where something went wrong and changed for the worse. So that's a good place to start. Examine the book's societal structure, the core of what's different about that society or government. Survival, too. How is it represented? Described? Break down the hardships, the descriptions of the weather and culture.

Romance is all about... well... romance. So that's where you focus. Start with the relationship, focus in on how the characters interact with each other, how are the emotions portrayed, when does your stomach flip in anticipation of a kiss?

Or what about historical fiction? Historical defines itself by the fact it's not set in modern-day times. The era it's set in is important because it changes the type of historical novel. How representative is the story and setting of that period in time? That's where you start. Dig into the setting, clothes, language the characters use. What about the food and tools the characters eat and use? Why and how does it feel different to modern day?

You literally can't have a historical novel set in modern times. She says... and promptly halts typing to think about the 1996 DiCaprio version of *Romeo and Juliet*, which was quite literally the historical story with historical language but set in the modern day...

Opens mouth to speak

Shuts it

Dust bunny rolls across the page

Well, anyway, I guess the point is that there are always exceptions to the rules, and these exceptions can periodically blur lines and create new genres.

Don't get pissy, I didn't make the rules.

I don't even like rules.

The problem is when you look at an outlier as an industry standard instead of what it really is: a one in a billion win.

This is going to hurt. Frankly, my fragile little ego can scarcely bring myself to write it. But the chances of you or I being the one in a billion are... well... one in a billion. Pretty fucking low odds. Which is why, much as none of us want to accept it, we probably ought to swallow the fact we're unlikely to be outliers. But that doesn't mean we can't have a bucket load of success and wins. It does mean we should all put the outliers down and focus on the meat of a genre.

Mmkay? Good.

How to Determine Genre

Perhaps the easiest way is to look at a society or organization's definition of their particular genre and take that on board. Google it. Wikipedia it.

The more time-consuming method would be to roll up your proverbial sleeves and drown in a genre-based to-be-read pile. Here, you can get a little woo-woo. Absorb as many books as you can, roll around in bed with them until you can reel off all the ways they're similar.

I've always thought one of the best questions to ask is why does a reader read that specific genre? Of course, this isn't going to get you an ironclad definition of a genre, but it is going to give you data on what's important to the readers of that genre.

How else can you determine what's genre and what's just a trope or literary mechanism? Patterns people, a bit of common sense, and consuming so many sodding books, your sixth sense tingles with pleasure every time you find a book in your genre.

Seriously though, scour say, five to ten books in one genre, what are the commonalities? Is it tone? Is it the same "totes emosh" feeling you have at the end? In epic fantasy, is it linguistics and levels of description? Or perhaps the vast landscapes they're all set in. For romance, is it the yearning the characters feel? Is it the similar plot beat structures? The fact the core is about a romantic relationship? Unlike Epic fantasy, it's not the setting. There are romances set in western locations, small towns, paranormal cities, alien spaceships, forests, and fantasy worlds.

Another aspect to consider is how do these similarities change over time? Because they do, this creates the wax and wane of trends. It's also why continuing to read in your genre is so important.

Genre at its core is fixed. At the edges, it breaks down into subgenres, niches, and trends.

Trends change.

My kid loves toast. If a genre were a piece of toast, then toast is always toast. It's *always* grilled bread. If you don't toast it, then it's bread. But what the kid *wants on* toast changes. Sometimes plain old butter is popular (think trend). Sometimes the kid wants butter and peanut butter (a similar but slightly different trend). And sometimes he'll go wild and have butter, peanut butter, and jelly on top (a really niche trend). But throughout these toast related fads, the thing that doesn't change is genre... aka the fact that it's the toast he wants.

STEP 1 READ SUMMARY

Where we filled our eyeballs with glitter crack, discussed the fact Stephen King is wrong, pondered our fragile little egos, tripped off our tits, and considered why we should all bash more coconuts.

- People are resistant to reading like a writer for two reasons:

1. They fear it will detract from their love of reading.
2. It skirts a little too close to comparison.

- When reading and deconstructing, I look at an author's work *not* to establish who is better or worse. But merely to examine the differences and similarities between their work and mine. That's it.
- As a "reader" when you read, it's usually unconscious, and thus forms a shallower level of reading. Your brain loses itself in the plot and therefore you only get the "what" of the story.

There are two types that we care about:

- Reading like a reader.
- Reading like a writer.

- How much data do you need to make a decision? That's how many books you need to read.
- If your goal is to pick up tools and devices from a book, then there's a deep-dive analytical deconstruction where you read one book deeply.
- If you want a comparative type of reading suited to understanding and knowing a genre, you need to read more than one book.
- Imitation *is* iteration.
- Methods for choosing books include: genre comparison authors, outside your genre, learning specificity, seminal genre works.
- A comparison author is an author who writes in the same genre AND sub niche as you. Their books have similar themes, tropes, or settings.
- Find comp authors via eBook categories, "Also Bought" sections, author profiles, bookstagram and genre specific podcasts.
- Genre indicates a certain 'style', a grouping. A selection of characteristics found in a group of books that denote a particular style. "Characteristics" being elements like tone, content, settings, level of steam, etc.

INTERMISSION

You've already picked your first book, but now I'm going to encourage you to create a short list of books you'd like to deconstruct over the next few months.

Hit up your local store, buy digital, tap your library, nab copies from friends. Whatever you do, create your pile and get ready to dive vagina-deep into deconstruction.

Second, it's time to read.

As you read the next step and learn how to deconstruct, start the first book you chose. Go steady. See what you can find in the first chapter. I think the first page is often critical. The author spends a lot of time on it and there are usually a dozen gems to unearth.

Read chapter one. Read it again. Dig deep.

Often, I find most of my tabs are in the earlier chunks of books and then again in the later chapters. Not always the case, especially if I'm reading for story structure. But if I'm just meandering through a casual read, that is usually the pattern. I always wondered if it's because once I reach the middle I'm so engaged with the story it's harder to pull myself out. And maybe that's why. But I think it's also because most of us spend a disproportionate amount of time working on the beginning of a book and therefore it's the densest area of tools and devices. You may find you have the same experience, or you might find your focus lies somewhere else.

STEP 2 DECONSTRUCTION

2.0 DECONSTRUCTION

Where we piss off Marie Kondo, vomit questions, get forensic with words, hack shit up, and find holy grails.

Here is where we really get down and dirty. Deconstruction is actually pattern recognition. We're going to take the words we read and smash them apart Hulk-style. Word-brick by word-brick we're going to pull sentences and paragraphs apart until we can scalpel out a single word, a single comma, so that we know and understand how the authors have created the mastery they've made.

This is a microscopic level of wordery. Then we're going to step back and work our way up and out to the bird's eye view of story and structure.

I want to manage expectations. There are so many elements of story, so many cells and fibers that go into making a complete book that to comment on how to deconstruct every thread would take a set of encyclopedic-length volumes. But I hope this section provides enough examples to help you either use these methods or figure out something that works better for you. I'm giving you a formula and structure for a process. My aim is to show you a method in sufficient detail you can confidently apply it to other aspects of deconstruction.

One more thing.

You have permission to disagree with my deconstruction or find other nuggets of gold from the examples I use that I didn't spot. Remember, we're all coming at this with our own lens of experience on. Each of us has a desire to find particular things, and we all have preferences for certain voices and techniques. I want you to hold on to that and encourage it. Your style will differ from mine, and unless you're trying to cozy up in the same genre of fiction I'm writing in, then we're probably going to want to look for different tools and devices, anyway.

If you pick up tools I don't in the next sections, that's a good thing. Keep them, cuddle and cultivate them, it will help you grow your own formula for working with books. And if you don't, then perhaps this will be the start for you.

Why Bother Deconstructing?

Alright look, I've used the house and architect analogy before, so let's bring that bad boy back into play. Let's say you're looking at this dream mansion you want to re-create in your style to live in as your forever home. You've looked at it, and the builder turns to you and says, right go on then and hands you the keys to a forklift truck.

That's basically what you're doing when you do nothing more than straight reads of books and expect yourself to write a best seller.

Groans

You can't look at a mansion and build one yourself any more than you can read a book and expect to write a smash hit.

No, darlings. You need to deconstruct it to understand how

the chapters flow together, the anatomy of a hook, and the elements that create a character. You need to break down the rhythm of a sentence so you can understand cadence and how the cement of punctuation creates the bricks of beats.

Deconstruction gives you both the tools and an instruction manual. It creates an entirely individualized manual because you'll only pull out the tools and devices you find attractive. If you don't like something, disregard it. You'll become your own writing coach.

The Art of Deconstruction

At the heart of deconstruction is curiosity. When I first started doing this, I didn't know I was "deconstructing". I just thought I was nosy and trying to figure out how and why the author I was reading was so annoyingly brilliant. And I was being nosy, but I was also deconstructing.

At its heart, deconstruction is literally asking questions.

Being curious and trying to ferret down into the character and sentences until you find the diamond that made this element of the best seller work.

Anyone can ask questions. But good deconstruction is about asking the right questions. Knowing how to be curious and what questions will elicit the information you're after. It's about looking at best sellers in a new light. It's also about pattern recognition and keeping shit simple.

I remember when I was a teen and in the army cadets. Once you reached Lance Corporal, you had to teach the kids below you. So you went on a course to learn how to teach. I still remember our Company Sergeant Major bellowing at the top of his very mustached lungs, "everyone needs to KISS". Of course, shouting that at a room full of hormonal teens only elicited a bout of giggling and whispers. Which, looking back, was the point. We paid attention, and I didn't forget the lesson.

He didn't want us to *actually* kiss. KISS stood for keep it simple, stupid.

And that, I think, is the most important lesson I've learned from deconstructing best sellers. Never look for a complicated formula. The vast majority of the time, the best answer is the simplest. One brick, one tool, one trick.

Break. It. Down.

Keep breaking it down until you can identify the simplest possible unit or tool. I'll give examples of this shortly.

Okay, enough talk, let's do this...

2.1 THUNDERBIRDS ARE GO...

"Marking a book is literally an expression of your differences or your agreements with the author. It is the highest respect you can pay him." Mortimer Adler, *How to Read a Book*.

Okay, here is a brief overview of the process I use. We are, of course, going to dive into much more detail as we go through this section. But for now, here's a bish-bash-bosh, wham, bam, thank you ma'am overview of the process.

Step 1: Feel the Feels

How do you even start trying to find tools in fiction? What do you look for? How do you know it's any good?

It depends.

It depends on how you interact with fiction now and how easy it is for you to separate out the experience from your observations. Your experience of the book and story will inform your observations. That is where you start.

If you've hung around me for any amount of time, you'll know I like to joke about being dead on the inside. Now, for the sake of my pride, I'd like you to pretend I skipped this part in the process—I didn't, but let's pretend, mmkay?

Right.

Step 1: Before you dip your fingers into the nitty-gritty of a novel and pull it apart, simply observe your experience. Let me say that again because it's important. Change nothing.

Just observe your experience of reading.

I want you to pick up a book you chose from one of your go-to authors and read it. And while you're reading it, I want you to notice how you feel. How you interact with the book.

Notice when you laugh, or smile, or swoon. Notice when you're pulled out of the story. When you're so swept away you don't hear your name being called. Or when your eyes switch off and your imagination takes over and pictures and landscapes roll over your vision.

Notice these things.

That's it.

Step 2: Mark When You Feel

Once you've done that, I want you to pick up another book by another one of your go-to authors. This time, when you feel something, I want you to stop. It doesn't matter whether you laughed, or smiled, swooned at the imagery or relationship. Whatever made you feel something, stop and go back. Reread the paragraph or two before you realized you were feeling something.

Highlight it, mark it, sticky tab it, rub yourself over it. Smear asterisks and pen marks, coffee stains, and chocolate daubs. It's your book. You own that motherfucker.

Be brave, write notes in the margins about what you feel, think, and are reflecting on. I know, I know, not everyone wants to mark a book. I'm pretty sure at least three people just had a heart attack, 38 percent of you are now sweating, and I've mortally offended at least one die hard must-keep-the-book-pristine reader.

Oops?

If you're reading digitally, it is perhaps an easier task, especially on a device that will allow you to handwrite on documents. But if you're a paperback reader, this is either going to be sacrilege, or the permission you needed. If you really can't drop a sticky note or slip of paper in where you had thoughts, then unless you have a photographic memory, chances are whatever you thought or felt in the moment will be lost later through the fog of screaming kids, shitty boss demands, and caffeine haze.

Write. It. Down.

When you tab or underline, you're only marking the "what" of what's caught your attention. You need to note why, too.

Did you think the author made an interesting choice? Was there a quirky metaphor? Did you laugh out loud?

Write. It. Down.

Did a specific question pop into your mind about something the author has done? Do you, at the moment, desperately want to know XYZ?

Write. It. Down.

Did you have an ah-ha and figure out exactly how the author did it while reading? *Pulls face* I swear to literary Jesus, if you don't write it down, I will come for you.

If nothing else, when you come back to review later, you'll thank me. Often these notes form the basis of ideas or new sentences you want to include in your own work.

Once you've gotten good at realizing you're not dead inside, but can thrust yourself into the swells of an emotional reaction to inanimate 2D characters created from ink and dead trees, you can take this a step further.

Rather than *stopping* when you feel something, stop and examine when you feel curious as a writer, too. Reacting emotionally to a story is still a reader reaction. To go deeper into the mechanics of the book, notice when you feel wonder as a writer. Ever read something and gone:

"Wow, I'd kill to write like that."

Bam.

Stop reading, underline that sucker.

Stop when you're in awe of what a writer did. Stop when the spite reflux gets going and you're considering which poison might work most effectively. Stop because you're inspired and in awe and utterly puzzled at how the author created such word wizardry. That's when you've got your author head on and that's when you'll mine gold.

Step 3: Analyze

It's entirely up to you when you do this, but the next step is analysis. For me, I like to stop while reading and try to work out what it was about the writing that made me feel something, but for others who enjoy powering through a story, you might not want to do this until you've finished the book. I'm going to spend entire sections looking at how to do the analysis, so I won't say more here, other than this is the next step.

Step 4: Develop Awareness

The aim of this practice is to develop the observation muscle. Start with the low hanging fruit. When you feel something in a story, it's pretty obvious. But once you've established that muscle, you need to flex it and push it harder so that you're able to notice other aspects of writing. Instances where you don't feel anything, but the writer is doing something clever, like dropping red herrings or foreshadowing.

Here, you can decide what you want to look for before reading. Let's say your inciting incidents in your novels are weak. If you go into a book knowing you want to improve your inciting incident, then you can be on the lookout for it in the books you read. If you've done any kind of craft research or reading, then you'll know the inciting incident appears around the 10-25 percent mark. It might not make you feel anything, but once your observation muscle is developed, spotting what you're after will be easier.

Read Every Single Word

One last point on the basic steps before we go deeper. I know lots of people like to read fast enough they either skim read, speed read or some other mechanism of powering through books. That's fine if you're reading for pleasure. But unless you have a superhuman skill to read fast and still spot all the tools a writer is using, then I'd recommend reading every single word when deconstructing. It's too easy to miss the vital parts of sentences. If you can skim and still take in every single word, then have a gold star. You get to feel like a smug bitch.

The point of reading every single word is to get a better sense of the rhythm and flow of the sentences. The more you're able to pick up nuances of word choice, even examine whether grammar and punctuation are having an effect or pick up on subtext you might've missed on first reading, the better.

Selling Shares in Sticky Tabs

I'm about to make some people squirm. I'm also a huge hypocrite, because while I will ardently refuse to bend or snap the spines of my books, I will happily adorn the pages with pencil notes and highlights. For me, there's nothing worse than finding an amazing passage in a book or a fantastic piece of dialogue and then putting your book down and never being able to find it again.

If that's making your book-bits hurt, then there's another way. First up, most e-reading devices have the functionality for you to take notes on your highlights and to export them. But if you're an old-skool reader like me and prefer paperback, then you can use a sticky tab system. I buy packets of sticky tabs in the thousands and they're usually sets of the same colors. Something standard like: pink, orange, yellow, green, blue, and a couple of variations of purple.

I assign meanings to the colors of the tabs so that when I finish, usually the book is smothered in one particular color more than the others and I can visually tell what that book did well from a glance.

If it helps, this is the system I use:

- Pink: character tools
- Orange: obvious tools such as foreshadowing, subtext, something structure related
- Yellow: narration / voice
- Green: description
- Blue: dialogue
- Purple: relationship
- Other purple: emotion and anything else

2.2 WHEN TO HALT... AND DO NOT PASS GO

Alright, this all sounds swell and all, a paragraph makes you feel something, but so what? How do you know when it's worth noting? The purpose of the following questions and points is to help you become more aware while reading. To help you consider the kinds of sentences and sections that may have tools and techniques buried inside. There's no guarantee, of course, but these are the stop and think moments that have led me to find tools and techniques.

I'm covering five areas as a starter: dialogue, description, characterization, technical observations, and sentence level observations. I'd recommend either brainstorming questions for areas you want to improve on or, as you pick things up in the books you're reading, note down the things that make you stop and why.

General "Rules" for Knowing When to Stop and Deconstruct

Rules?
God, I felt dirty writing the word "rules" *shudders* I did it

again. Look, let's just move on before I shit the bed and can't write the rest of this section.

Two things. First, remember that if you feel something for the characters or plot, then it's worth stopping and going back to see what happened in the last paragraph and page. To elicit an emotion, authors do a lot of the work in the setup. Setup is sometimes immediately before the line that elicits emotion or it could be further back. If it's new to you, use it. There will be a tool or tactic buried in the sentence you've not seen before, which means there's something handy in there to dig up.

When reading good books, there is a desire to find the most important sentences, the key line that breaks the book apart and gives you the recipe to Frankenstein your own best seller. And yes, there will be some sentences that structurally give you the goods. Like the revelation during the dark night of the soul. This is the scene in a story with the darkest emotional moments. Perhaps the mentor dies, or the hero believes there's no way to win. Whatever takes the hero to this place, it's always the "lowest" or "darkest" moment in the book, usually around 75 percent of the way through.

Other places where you might find an important sentence could be the inciting incident or the final scene where there's a "lesson learned". But unless you're actively trying to deconstruct for story structure (which is a valid exercise, by the way), then it *almost* doesn't matter what you underline or pick out.

Why?

Because what's important to *you* in the book won't reflect what was important to the author at the time of writing. We can't know what the author's favorite lines are. We can't know for sure whether what they created was conscious or if it was the genius workings of their subconscious.

We can only know what is, what is in front of us, and what is important to our souls. So don't overthink the underlining process. Once an author finishes a book and pushes it out into the world, it's no longer theirs. Each book is the property of the purchaser, the reader, the consumer of its words. Not the creator. The creator only owns it while it's being created. Strange, really, to think that as I sit here and type this sentence, the book is still mine. But once you are reading this sentence, the book will already be yours.

Each reader has their own fetish flavor of book. They read, interact, and absorb story in their own way, with their own lens and rose-tinted spectacles.

If you've been writing—or reading—for any amount of time, then you innately know story. You know it in your genetic coding, in your bones and your heart. You'll feel your way to the important lines, because they're important to you. That tells you something. It tells you to deconstruct that line because it's going to give you a tool you'll want to use.

Ultimately, to be curious is to be creative, to be clever, and to craft your own mastery.

Here are a few ideas to help you spot words, sentences, and tools an author uses.

Dialogue

When and why I note dialogue:

- A line of dialogue shocks me.
- A line or a section of dialogue makes me laugh.
- It makes me cry.
- There was an amazing insult.
- The back and forth felt realistic.
- I was dying over an argument and screaming in frustration.
- I felt basically anything.
- The character's voice was so unique and I could "hear" it.

Description

When and why I note description:

- Something created vivid images for me, or I pictured the scene in detail.
- I found myself lost, day-dreaming or forgetting the real world exists because I'm in an amazing fantasy world.
- Something evoked a memory, or smell for me.
- The author is describing the world or building or situation, but I gained an unexpected insight into a character.
- I can practically smell/feel/hear the world.
- I find I long to go to the place described.
- The author describes something unusual, or the description is unusual.
- The description makes me go "wow" either for prose or imagery.

Characterization

When and why I note character and characterization:

- The character is quirky in looks, behavior, attire, or personality.
- I'm surprised or shocked by the character in some way.
- An internal thought showed me a new insight into the protagonist.
- The character's voice is utterly unique and memorable.
- The character said or did something that gave me an insight into another character.

- A character made an observation or noticed a detail that I found surprising or insightful.
- The character's philosophical viewpoint made me think differently about life.
- The character had an unusual habit, quirk, or action that was unexpected or unusual.

Technical Observations

When and why I note technical observations:

- I noticed a piece of foreshadowing.
- Something made me guess at the ending of the book or an impending twist.
- I saw an effective juxtaposition, simile, metaphor… insert other device.
- The author broke a writing rule like using an adverb, but I loved the way they styled it out, anyway.
- Maybe I noticed some alliteration that made a sentence flow beautifully.
- The author personified the weather.
- There is a revelation at exactly the halfway point of the book that felt impactful.
- The dark night of the soul really hit home for me.
- Something shocked me or took me unawares, perhaps a plot twist that "made sense" even though I didn't see it coming. A reread under these circumstances can be most fruitful, as you can keep a lookout for clues the second time around.

Sentence Level Observations

Sentence level observations are about as detailed as you can get. Think monkey-evil-eyeing-a-nit-in-your-scalp level of detail. But when and why do I note sentence level observations?

- The author did something technical I haven't seen before.
- They employed footnotes to create voice or quirky narration.
- The author uses unusual sentence structures and grammar. Perhaps a parenthesis or an asterisk.
- There is something unusual about the rhythm of a sentence that caught my eye.
- They used em dashes to add extra insight or break complex sentences down and this told me something about a character.
- Something was unexpected or out of the ordinary.
- The author did something at the sentence level that I've never seen before.
- The book's format was different.
- Something about the sentence level style changed or affected my interaction with the story or characters.

2.3 THE ART OF THE QUESTION

Half of the difficulty of deconstructing a best seller comes from not knowing how to, well, deconstruct. I don't know how other authors do it, but for me, it's all about the question. More specifically, being artful with questions.

Ask, ask, ask.

You know the whiny three-year-old's who cause trauma twitches... sorry, tremors in your eyeballs from their incessant use of the word, why? Weeell, how do you feel about becoming that kid?

Now let me caveat that, because a kid just asking an unrelenting series of "why's" is liable to get punched in the face...

Silence

Sacha fidgets in her throne under the weight of the reader's side eye

That was too much, wasn't it? I went too far this time.

Note to self, joking about punching innocent kids in the face is not, in fact, funny.

Right, to figure out what the author has done with the sentence, paragraph, scene or otherwise that you're analyzing, ask a metric fuckload of questions. But not just any questions, really sodding specific ones. The more specific you are, the sharper the spade you dig with and the more acute the discoveries you'll make.

Why did they use that specific word? Why did they use a juxtaposition in that metaphor? Why does subversion work here? What kind of personification did they use? How did the punctuation affect the flow and rhythm?

On and on it goes.

Think like a journalist. Journos love a bit of the five 'Ws': who, when, what, why, where and usually, how thrown in for good measure. In book terms, when and where are usually the same. Nevertheless, embody your inner journo and get comfy with these questions. They'll help you break down everything an author has done.

Let's take each in turn.

Who: who is saying what you're reading? Protagonist, narrator, side character? Someone else?

When: when is this passage in the book? Does the placement mean something? Is it in an emotional scene? Does it correlate with a pivotal story structure moment? i.e., inciting incident, dark night of the soul, the climax etc.

What: what is it? Description, dialogue, narrative summary, inner thought, personification, a juxtaposition, subversion, characterization? What device or tool is the author using?

Why: why did they use that specific tool? Was it to make you feel a certain way? To reveal information? To make you empathize with an awful character? To draw glorious rainbow-colored images in your mind? To make something resonate? Why was this moment in particular powerful?

How: this is the tricky bit. This is where you understand what the author has done. How did the author create the effect? Combine the answers to all the other questions and dig to the simplest unit to discover the how.

Ws are good, but they're not the only question. Let's look at some more questions you can ask. Those five Ws and an H are the foundation of all questions. Slap them out whenever takes your fancy. But there are other angles you can bend your questioning around too.

If you would like to see examples of this analysis in practice, you can download my free bonus cheat sheet by visiting: sach ablack.co.uk/bestseller

Let's furrow deeper.

Stick it in. Pull it Out...

Have you ever gotten confused by reading a book? Maybe you lose sight of whose limbs are whose in a battle scene or you didn't quite understand the description you just read. Those are good places to stop and ask yourself what was confusing about it? Where did you lose the thread, and why and what could the author have done differently?

Regardless of whether you liked or disliked a piece of writing, when you have a "feeling" about it, it's a good time to stop. Why was the piece effective or not? Thinking purely in terms of like and dislike is a good start, but it keeps your thinking inward. Considering only how *you* feel. Scrutinizing whether the writing was effective is a more outward approach. It will help you think about other readers and how you consider them in your own writing. We have to whip our inner diva out to discover what she feels strongly about, and then smack her tushy back inside so the big girls can do the analysis. Consider why something was effective. Did the author use appropriate or inappropriate language?

Sex scenes are a great place to start because they're either done really well or they're so squicky and icky they make you squirm. But it's abundantly obvious when an author has messed up.

For example, let's say an author used the word vagina in a sex scene... Maybe the author wrote, "he plunged his penis into her vagina."

Oh. My... I can't believe I actually wrote that.

Do you feel gross?

I feel like I just violated my eyeballs typing that. I apologize. But it made my point. I'm not sure I have to explain why that is not an effective or appropriate choice of wording for a bedroom romp. Description in sex scenes is about insinuation and innuendo. Plus "vagina" and "penis" are anatomical, scientific names—at no point in history has anyone ever said those words sounded sexy. And it's definitely not something that's going to get your everyday reader hot under the collar. So neither word was appropriate and the only thing it was effective for was turning the reader off. When you consider what's effective, you look outward, you consider your dear reader's sensibilities and what will have the greatest impact on them.

And speaking of audience...

Intended Munchkins

One short word on considering who the author's intended audience is. Why is this even relevant? It adds another layer to "appropriate". There's appropriate word choice to create effective description, and then there's appropriateness for "genre" or even "age" too.

All of this should lead you to asking...

WWYD?

What would you do?

How would you change what the author did to make it better or different? Asking this forces you to consider the author's choices and how they affected the reader, your reader. It also makes you consider the quality of the writing and if you're able to form an opinion, then you can recognize what's good and perhaps what's not. That means you can apply that knowledge to your own work and decide what you do and don't want to see.

And speaking of what you want to see...

The Prediction Game

Do you ever sit with your spouse, family member, house-mate, or by yourself while watching TV or a movie and play the prediction game? Do you spout guess after guess about who the killer is, how the love interest will do the grand romantic gesture, or what the secret is the side character is keeping? I'm going to assume most of you said yes, because who doesn't do that? But if you don't, it's time to kick the Sherlocking up to the next level.

Do What I Say Not What I Do

Then there's the other type of question to ask. Or perhaps an action to spot. When a character says one thing, but does something else, it's time to stop and figure out what just happened. Whenever you feel the dissonance between what you're predicting or what you expected and what's actually happening, the author's had you, the devious little bastard. The author pulled the wool over your eyes and you need to figure out how.

2.4 OLYMPIC PATTERN SPOTTING

This is where we really piss off Marie Kondo. Instead of un-hauling all the books that we've read or no longer bring us joy, we hoard sentences and tabs like the author-monsters we are.

Unconscious Genius

I feel like here is a good place to stop and talk about some-thing awkward before we dive into too much detail on the deconstruction. Some of you will think... but I don't put any of this genius stuff into my prose. I just write shit and it makes a book.

I know. That's okay.

But just cause an author isn't putting this stuff in intention-ally, doesn't mean they're not doing it at all. Writers spend years honing their craft, so yes, some patterns we dig up, some of the foreshadowing or the intricate symbolism was left there uncon-sciously for the reader to discover and absorb. Let's go back to the archaeologists. It's the difference between accidentally digging up a dinosaur bone that was left in the exact place it died, and excavating an Egyptian tomb that was built and buried in a known Egyptian town. Both valid, both exist, but one was done intentionally and the other just happened.

Does this mean that you're going to have to use all the tools you find intentionally? And write in a really rigid intentional manner? I think you know the answer to that.

Like any kind of learning, once you have consolidated it, it becomes a skill you can use over and over. Just like driving.

Sticky Tab Heaven

Once you've finished reading a book, there's probably going to be seventy-eight thousand sticky tabs adorning the pages. I won't lie. My house is the house where sticky tabs come to die. Sorry for any sticky tab aficionados out there, but my home is a sacrificial hellmouth that regularly swallows mountains of the little fuckers up.

Why am I talking about tabs again?

When your book has that many underlines and notes, it can be a little overwhelming knowing where to start with analysis.

But see, young tab-wan, the stickies are the easiest place to start... IF and only if you've tabbed systematically. I'm referencing the color-coded tab system I suggested in 2.1.

If each colored tab always means the same thing, then before you go to review your margin scribbles, take a quick look at your book's edge.

This will give you data and a guide for what to focus on before you even open the front cover to review your notes.

For example, I can tell you that my copy of *The Ten Thousand Doors of January* by Alix E. Harrow has mostly green tabs (for description). My copy of *The Hating Game* by Sally Thorne mostly has purple for romance and relationships. My copy of *The House in the Cerulean Sea* by T. J. Klune mostly has blue dialogue tabs. Before I even open those books to review my notes, I have a direction. There's something about Alix's description I must have found appealing. Therefore, I should focus my thoughts and analysis there. Likewise, but for Sally's relationship building and ditto for Klune's dialogue.

What if you don't have an overriding color?

Don't worry, maybe the author is an all-rounder, or there were lots of different things to love... or maybe it was just a shit book.

Captain Review

I don't know how you learn, and a lot of building this system will depend on what you know already works for you. If you already have systems that work, use them, keep them, don't for the love of literary gods, change them.

When I started reading like this, I wrote up all the quotes digitally and put them into meaningful sections. I had to "see" the quotes all together to work out what the patterns were. I don't need to do that so much now for a couple of reasons.

- I'm better at writing more comprehensive notes in the margin.
- I'm a faster reader and try to get through a book in a couple of days, meaning I can hold the information temporarily in my mind, which allows me to reflect and review on what the author has done and spot patterns mentally.
- When I read, I'm consciously looking for patterns, which makes it easier to spot.

But for those coming to this for the first time, you need to create your own review method. Maybe you need to write them up by hand, maybe you can export the digital notes and collate them, move them around, or simply read them again. I've even tried printing them out, cutting them up and dropping them into piles... Yes, I experimented a lot when I first started doing this.

What you want is to get to a position where you can see or easily review just your notes and the quotes you've highlighted. It often helps to go back to the beginning of the book and reread all the sentences you've underlined and the notes you've written, ignoring everything else. Doing that in a short space of time will allow you to hold the information in your head long enough to spot patterns between your highlights.

If you don't sticky tab, then think about the book. What was the element or aspect of their writing you enjoyed most? Did something stand out? What made you feel things? Did you find yourself lost in a rich world of imagery, or maybe squealing about a relationship?

Start with excellence. Deconstruct that. Then, if you fancy doing another aspect of the book, have at it. Otherwise, move on and find the next author with a streak of excellence.

P... P... Pattern Recognition

Step 1: Collect sentences
Step 2: Organize sentences
Step 3: Ask questions about sentences
Step 4: Imagine what else you can do with what you found

So we have a cluster of highlights and tabs and underlines. Now what?

Whether you're an Einstein-like math and physics geek or a word nerd, our minds and bodies are biologically wired to seek out patterns. As children, our brains develop mental boxes—

called heuristics—that enable us to group similar items together for comparison and definition. In other words, pattern recognition. For example, a square will be in the square heuristic. Regardless of whether it's big or small, yellow, dotty, patterned or has transparent innards: a square is a square. The brain figures this out by comparing all squares together and identifying the similarities and differences.

Thus, pattern spotting in literature is also about finding the similarities and differences between elements of the stories.

But how do we make this easy for ourselves?

Look, I don't want to sound negative, but I will do most things for spite. And I'm betting a fair few of you would, too. I reckon there's two ways to begin. Take your highlights and look for what you love, or look for what you hate. Either way, those will be the things most salient to you because they're most obvious. Chances are, the things you hate are easier to spot because they have the added extra of providing a knee jerk irritation.

I start the process by looking for anything I love or hate that the author does repeatedly. For example, an author who consistently writes gorgeous metaphors. Or highlights where the character description is quirky. Then when I have a cluster of examples, I go deeper. Look for repetition. A repeating technique, rhythm, word choice. What is similar in those instances and what is different?

How do the words interact with each other? How are the things you've highlighted structured?

Cause and effect, baby.

You're looking for the words, tools, structures, or devices that caused the effect you felt as a reader. Connections, relationships between words and grammar. Between paragraphs and scenes. This is where we question what the writer has done. Then we imagine what else they could have done or what we, ourselves, can do instead.

Know Shit About Story and Stuff

There are two sides to this deconstruction coin. There's the "let's see what I can dig up and the patterns I find" side. And the "what standard story devices and structures are in use?"

This is the portion of the book where we reach a paradox. The more you know about story, structure, how to characterize effectively, etc., the easier it is to spot that element in a story. If you innately know how to create that yourself, then you can spot it in someone else's work. However, deconstruction is literally the act of discovering and knowing things you didn't know you could know.

Anyone else have to reread that sentence?

Can you come at deconstruction having learned nothing about story structure or how to write a book? Of course, but paradoxically, knowing some stuff will help you discover more stuff. It's like having a map that gets you 75 percent of the way to the finish line.

Let's say you don't know what filtering is. It's unlikely you'll spot it in a story.

Briefly, filtering is when the author uses unnecessary filler words to remove the reader one step from the character. For example, nine times out of ten you can remove the words "she felt, he heard, she saw" and the sentence retains the same meaning. For more on this and other ways to improve your sentence level writing, refer to my other book, *The Anatomy of Prose.*

However, once you know what filtering is, you can't un-know it. Which means you're always able to spot it in fiction. That said, maybe in reading lots of work, a different writer discovered that sometimes sentences are fuller and clunkier and didn't have a name for it, but "felt" like they could remove those words. It feels all chicken and egg to me, which is why I mix and match my learning.

Do you have to learn everything about craft before you start deconstruction? No. But arming yourself with literary language and craft knowledge helps you spot tools faster than if you come at it with a baseline of zero. Get comfy understanding the difference between a plot point and the inciting incident, be one with scene anchoring versus chapter hooks.

2.5 DISTILLING TO THE SIMPLEST UNIT

We're word players, right? We like frolicking in the word pit. Smearing chocolaty word goodness over our boobs and motorboat...

Wait.

Wrong book.

We like words, right?

Good.

Here is where you need to create your own language. The art of really mastering deconstruction is to drill down to—not necessarily the smallest unit you find, but the **simplest**.

I'll say that again, cause it's crucial.

Good deconstruction drills down to the simplest unit possible.

There, in the microcosm of wordery, you'll find tools. But in order to identify the tools, you need to name them. Language is communication. It's our primary resource and we need it if we're going to identify the devices we find.

I'm sure there are lots of official, prim and proper grammatically excellent terms for all these tools and stuff, but...

Well, we all know how I feel about rules.

So fuck that, fuck this, and fuck the other.

Make it up.

Your job as a writer is quite literally to make shit up. Look, no one else is going to see your deconstruction... Unless you're me and sharing your literal process.

When I break down what an author is doing, I need to point at a "thing" and say she's doing that. He did this.

"This, that" and "thing" aren't exactly useful identifiers. Not if you want to understand your notes and implement later. You need your own language and words. Because you know what? Once you've spotted a tool, you'll see it everywhere and you can't be calling the tools you find thingamajigs, whatsitbobs, and jigglebums...

Let's look at an example. I loved *The Invisible Life of Addie LaRue* by V. E. Schwab. Something I'd noticed in other books but hadn't been able to pin down fully until I read her book was what I call "Intangible Tangible."

> "And there will be a moment, as brief as a yawn, where she won't know where she is."

So this was the sentence I underlined in her book. It's gorgeous and lyrical and I love it. More than that, I covet it. I want to write like that; I want to write better than that. Don't we all want to be as good as or better than the authors we admire? To do that, I have to work out what it is I love about the line and how the effect was created.

On the surface level, we could say okay, there's a rhythm to the sentence because of the punctuation. But that's not really it. "I loved this line for the punctuation," said literally no one ever.

So, is it the fact she's employed a simile coated with a bit of loose personification?

Well, yeah. But I can lob the words simile and personification around everywhere, but that doesn't help me create gorgeous prose like Schwab.

Yo, you there... writer person... can you whip out a simile for me?

Bet you can.

No, this is too high level of a view. It's not granular enough to see the threads of power in the sentence.

So let's go deeper. What is it about *this* simile that's so acutely mesmerizing?

"A moment, as brief as a yawn,"

What is a moment? It's a measure of time, but it's also undefinable. One person's "moment" is another's eon. Which means it's entirely undefinable. It's intangible. You can't hold it, you can't touch it, or feel it, or really capture what it is. But that is the purpose of a metaphor and simile. It turns something complex or difficult to explain and *know* into something entirely relatable. When it's relatable, we understand it, feel it, and breathe it. That's when we as authors connect with readers.

And that's exactly what Schwab does. She compares and connects an intangible "moment" to something that's entirely tangible and definable. Everyone yawns. We can all picture how long a yawn is. And I swear to god if I yawn again while writing this paragraph I'm going to throw my keyboard across the office.

The point is, what makes that simile spectacular is that she makes the intangible, tangible. That's the power.

"A moment [intangible], as brief as a yawn [tangible],"

To me, that is the simplest unit I could find. The easiest explanation. So let's call a spade a spade and the technique, henceforth, shall be known as *Intangible-Tangible*. Is there an official name or term to describe what this is? Maybe. Probably. But do I have any fucks left in my jar to give?

Absolutely not.

It doesn't matter whether there's an official term or word. It doesn't matter whether you're technically correct. What matters is your understanding. What matters is that you're empowered to break down the literary magic and take it for your own. Call it after your nanna, name the device after your favorite kink, or plant or literally anything. Identify the tools in a way that makes sense for you and enable you to replicate in your own work.

Fuck everyone else and their judgy "official" terminology.

Steps off soap box

Right, back to deconstruction. I bet you anything there are similes and metaphors and examples we can find that do the opposite of what we just found and instead do a *Tangible-Intangible*.

I reckon you can find an example where the author takes something knowable and tangible, a common everyday occurrence, and makes it special and interesting by relating it to something intangible. That's the twist on description I love to see. I can just imagine it would turn a common emotion or object into something universal and deep and spectacular.

And so, from one sentence, one observation, we have two techniques with an identifiable label that I just made up. And yes, I could use simile or personification as a label, but that doesn't capture the tool. I want my tool to say what it does on the tin. And I want you to create your own language around the tools you're discovering, too.

But What if it's Not a Tool?

There are instances where you might have highlighted something interesting, but there isn't a distinct label you can give it because it's less tool and more about the structure of what you've highlighted. What do I mean by that? Let's take the opening line from *Who I Was With Her* by Nita Tyndall.

"When I hear that she's dead, I run."

So this is a cracking line, especially a first line. But what do we think of it? What is it about the line that makes it so good? Especially because I don't really see a "tool". Let's look at the structure instead.

"When I hear that she's dead, I run."
Shocking revelation + unexpected character (re)action.

This works because there's an unexpected character reaction. But it's more than that. The structure of the sentence is key.

The first part of the sentence, structurally, is the setup for the later character reaction payoff. When "most" people hear that someone they love or care about has passed away, there's usually an emotional outburst, be it crying or shutting down and silence. A person running, though, is not expected. So, I suppose we could label this "unexpected character reaction" as the tool. But it feels like the simplest unit needs to include the setup to make sense because any character can react unexpectedly. Doesn't mean it lands correctly.

So, my language for this tool is the sentence above: shocking revelation + unexpected character (re)action.

2.6 SENTENCE LEVEL DECONSTRUCTION

When it comes to deconstruction, I like to break it down into micro, mid, and macro. This enables me to parse out distinct elements of story without overwhelming myself with the job. Let's start with micro.

What Counts as Micro-Level?

Well, my deconstruction munchkins, that's up to you. What do you deem sentence level and what do you feel is more character based? What does story structure mean to you? Remember the discussion about language and terminology?

Well, that.

So many story elements blend into each other that it's hard to have black and white edges. And frankly, I'm not sure it matters. What makes sense to you? What framework *feels* right? Are you a bum or boobs gal?

Enough waffling. What am I counting as sentence level?

- Anything that is granular
- Punctuation

- Devices like metaphors and similes
- Studying verbs
- Word choice
- Intentional repetition
- Footnotes or quirky formatting
- Unusual phrases or clauses
- Anything that is connected to words on a micro or granular level counts

Where this gets tricky is when the sentence is specifically depicting characterization. Say a metaphor that also shows me something important about the character's personality. Or perhaps a sentence that is also foreshadowing. It gets tangled, like juggling the limbs in a threesome. Here, I'd look at it with two hats on. First at the sentence level to see what forensic evidence I can pull out and then I stand back and examine what it's also telling me about character or story.

I start microscopic, always. Which means the words. When I'm done with words, I rise out of the ashy word-carcass until I'm looking at the sentence overview. Here I read the map from the phoenix's view. That's where I learn about the mid-level details. After that, I take another step back and see if I can spot anything else connecting to the story.

One last thing to note is that while I explain the differences in deconstructing story elements as three distinct parts, there's nothing to say you have to analyze in these at separate times. You may find that although you think of deconstruction in this way, you analyze all levels simultaneously—which is what I do.

Ding, Ding... Rereaders vs Analyze-As-You- Goers

In the left corner we have rereaders, in the right we have... no, I'm just kidding. This isn't a competition... But if it was, the best method would be...

Okay, okay, I'll stop.

If you're an analyze-on-the-first-read, like me, as opposed to a rereader, then you only get one shot at analysis. So you need a process for looking at all the information a book holds without overwhelming yourself.

Another way I like to think about pattern recognition in the books I read is to think of it as a triangle. Wide base at the bottom—this is the biggest picture information like story, arc, and theme. Step up into the middle of the triangle to look at character and scene level. At the top of the triangle, the peak, you have the smallest details, sentence level patterns, and variations. Depending on whether you like to work bottom up or top down, you can go either way.

For me, I don't enjoy reading spoilers or knowing the plot before I go in—that's part of why I loathe rereading. If I don't know the overarching plot before I start, I have no choice but to begin at the top of the triangle in the weeds and look at the detail of the book's sentences. It's only as I progress through the book that I gather enough information about the story and characters that I can see the bigger picture and, therefore, move down the triangle and analyze larger story elements. Thus, for me, it's easier to work top down—it's not that I'm a dictator and like being in charge or anything, you can work bottom up if you prefer. And, in fact, for rereaders, this might be an easier method for you as you're starting with the big picture plot already in mind.

But, to note a pattern... I've always thought rereaders were like plotters. They come to the analysis already knowing a huge chunk of information about the story. Which means, if you analyze as you go, you're more like an author who writes into the dark. That's not to say if you're a plotter, then you have to be a rereader, or if you're a pantser, then you have to analyze as you go. As if you'd think I'd be that prescriptive. Dahhhling, please, I just like the analogy.

What Does Sentence Level Deconstruction Look Like?

This is the sentence we're going to use.

"But already the edges were rubbing off the memory's freshness. I could feel it degrading in my hands." Melissa Albert, *The Hazel Wood.*

Sentence Level Analysis

The following three analysis quotes are all lifted from *The Anatomy of Prose.* This is the source of where this book came from, so I think it's only polite to make a nod to it. But I'm changing up how I structure the example to show you different deconstruction levels.

"I chose this sentence for a bazillion reasons, mostly it tickled my good bits. First of all, Albert takes an intangible concept— a memory—and makes it tangible. Hello device that I've already mentioned used in a different way... *Slides tool into literary knapsack*.

Albert also poses two juxtaposed words against each other: freshness and degrading. These two used in close proximity create a rich imagery effect in themselves.

Last, I wanted to pick up on the specific use of the word degrading. That single word choice created a picture in my mind where I could see a translucent orb in a hand with frayed edges and pieces breaking off in the wind."

Depending on how you look at story, sometimes you can't help but analyze up and out too, so here's how you could look at this sentence in reference to mid-level information.

Mid-Level Analysis

I don't want to go into too much detail about the other levels of analysis here. But for the sake of giving an example of complete deconstruction, here's a brief look at the other two layers.

Also, it won't always be the case that you can find other levels in a highlight. But here, there are some clear character observations to be made.

> "This sentence took a familiar concept—memory—and used it in a unique way to create characterization. Some of the most wonderful characterization comes from the details that only that character notices. In this instance, the character (Alice), notices how memories fade. Of course we all know memories fade, but it's the fact she draws attention to the detail of it degrading that shows insight into her character. It shows that memories have importance to her and that she pays attention to detail and the things that slip between. Which is funny, because the whole book is about fairytales slipping between worlds. The fact that Alice can feel a memory but more, feel it degrading also tells you she's special, magical, perhaps."

Macro-Level Observation

Not a lot to say here, other than from one sentence alone—unless it's connected to a plot point, such as a character's revelation after the dark night of the soul, or foreshadowing etc., then you're unlikely to draw much from it in relation to story structure or big picture observations. Big Cersei Lannister shame, shame, shame. But also very true.

Implementation

Again, implementation is an entire step in this book, so I

won't go into much detail here. But for the sake of a complete example, let's do it.

> "Instead of making memories as a concept tangible, you could turn an emotion into a tangible thing by describing the texture of how it feels. Rather than stating your character feels angry, you could describe the hot silk flame flowing beneath his ribcage, the flickering edges singeing his lungs and boiling his blood.
>
> Another way you might iterate the tool is instead of texture, use the method to give a memory or emotion a smell. I'm a total fangirl for smell in fiction because it's such an underused sense—but also smell is closely linked to memory, so it's super effective at creating imagery. This is a known cognitive phenomenon. The brain's structured so that smell neurons pass messages to each other very close to the area where your brain processes memory. The resulting effect is that you smell something and it evokes a memory. You know, like when you smell home cooked food in the street and you think of Sunday dinners at your mom's. I smell musty old books and instantly think of childhood. You could make your character's anger tangible by describing the scent of ash and burning rubber or perhaps the taste of hot bile in your prose. The options are limitless."

Taking this a step further, could you, instead of using the tool specifically, use the concept? What minor detail does your character notice that others don't? Can you find or pick something that connects to your story in the same way noticing the in-between did for Alice and the fairytales that moved between worlds? What she did is so delicious, I'm practically rubbing my hands on my thighs and cackling like a demon queen.

More Micro-Level Examples

Character Description

I had an insightful conversation with one of my favorite authors, Alix E. Harrow, on episode 133 of The Rebel Author Podcast. We talked about character description and how to create exquisite prose—something she does frequently. Alix said she doesn't follow a specific set of rules when writing. But for the quote I mentioned in the show, she did use a formula. The quote is the first line in her award-winning short story, *A Witch's Guide to Escape: A Practical Compendium of Portal Fantasies.*

"There have only ever been two kinds of librarians in the history of the world: the prudish, bitter ones with lipstick running into the cracks around their lips who believe the books are their personal property and patrons are dangerous delinquents come to steal them; and witches." Alix E. Harrow, *A Witch's Guide to Escape: A Practical Compendium of Portal Fantasies*—Apex Magazine #105 (February 2018)

Alix described the formula in the episode like this:

- "I can't ever have heard it before (the description)
- It has to tell me something specific about the person, not just the way they look
- That thing has to be true. And by true, I mean something that I myself have experienced in the world. A type of person that feels recognizable."

This is an unusual situation because we, as readers, don't normally get to hear the inner workings of an author's mind. But let's reverse engineer the quote and overlay the formula onto Alix's sentence.

It's obvious that the entire sentence is utterly unique. It's what caught my eye as I read her story. So I think that's covered point one. Point two, *that it tells us something specific and not just about a character's physicality*. Well, this sentence does both.

> "There have only ever been two kinds of librarians in the history of the world: the prudish, bitter ones with lipstick running into the cracks around their lips *[here is the physical description]* who believe the books are their personal property and patrons are dangerous delinquents come to steal them *[this tells us about who she is, what she believes, and the core of her personality]*; and witches."

And as for point three, who hasn't experienced a librarian like that? It's so delightfully true. Of course, there are many types of librarian, but I bet you've met one like this.

A Couple of Examples of Common Tools to "Where's Wally/Waldo"

There are many hundreds, if not thousands, of tools you could hunt for or discover yourself. So don't feel restricted. I'm not handcuffing you to this list. But here are a couple of examples of the more common tools writers use that count as easy opportunities to help train your deconstruction eye. Think of these as your Friday night fish and chips. If you want to find the caviar of tools, or more nuanced delicacies, it's over to you.

~

Tool: Punctuation play

Any occasion where an author messes with the punctuation of a sentence or paragraph. This could be by using excessive punctuation, creating a rhythm with repeating five-word sentences, for example, one-word sentences, or excessively long run-on sentences, etc.

What to look for: a sudden change in the pace of a story, usually found in highly charged scenes, emotional scenes, high tension.

Example

"Breath. Fingers. Lips. Tongues."

Like Thorne's use of single word sentences earlier, this creates a rapid staccato pace to the line. It's almost breathless with its beat. The rapid succession of full stops also creates rhythm in the line. And you can imagine the eyes, lips, or mouth roving across the character's body while stating the body parts. Another good example of punctuation play comes from Mike McCormack who wrote *Solar Bones*, a novel that is literally only one sentence long despite its 200+ pages.

What to break down

Oh, this could be endless. First up, what punctuation was (or was not) used? Did the author use a comma?—fucking comma-bastards-bane-of-my-existence... Did the author use a semicolon?—the pretentious clever bastard, not all of us can use them correctly. Or perhaps they intentionally underused the full stop? Maybe they employed an asterisk or five for foot-notery fun. Maybe they overused em dashes for asides—I don't know anyone who does that...

Do they use brackets in fiction? Heathens.

What type of punctuation is in play and what impact does that have on the flow of the sentence? Is it jarring? Does it flow like the emotion they're describing? Does it create a joke and punchline?

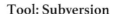

Tool: Subversion

Subversion means going against the expected. Doing something startling with your word choice or your descriptions. Blue skies, for example, are mundane. Everyone expects them to be described as blue. Break the rules, use juxtapositions, double meanings and shocking descriptions to create sharper imagery.

What to look for: a surprising description, something commonplace compared to something you'd never pair with it. Usually in description. But could easily be a tool for making character dialogue standout. You can also find it at the mid-level, a quirky habit, a character you expect to be one way and then is another. Settings with an unusual make up, etc.

Example

> "Beneath the beauty and the charm and the sharp sparkle of her personality, she had a core of steel. She was like a blade wrapped in a bouquet of orchids. I hoped to god whoever took her made the mistake of underestimating her." Melissa Albert, *The Hazel Wood.*

There's a couple of tools used here. First, subversion. You don't expect a personality to be described like this. It's so fresh. But we can dig deeper because Albert has used another tool to create this unexpected description. Juxtapositions. Two of them, in fact. The first is *"sharp sparkle"* sharp and sparkles are opposites of sorts. You don't expect to see them paired. Second, *"a blade wrapped in a bouquet of orchids."* Here, again, a blade is a sharp, violent object, and an orchid is soft and beautiful. Such a rich contrast between the two is both unexpected and a juxta-position.

What to break down

- The core of subversion is the unexpected. So that's the first place to dig for gold.
- What was it that was unexpected?
- Which words stuck out to you?
- Why did they stick out?
- Conversely, if something was surprising, then what were you expecting?
- Why did this subversion stick out?
- What made the contrast so sharp and the imagery so vivid?
- Did the author also use another tool, like a metaphor or simile?
- How did the imagery impact your opinion of the characters or the setting?
- Why do you think the author chose this moment to use subversion?
- What is important about what is being described?
- Could you create the same effect by substituting the two elements used?
- How could you change the sentence to make the subversion stronger? More impactful?
- Or perhaps what weaker words could you use to make it softer?
- Which words contrast with each other?

~

Tool: Fourth Wall Breaks

Oh, you have no idea how much I love this devious little puppy. Think Deadpool and Austin Powers. Fourth Wall breaks occur when the author speaks directly to the reader. Originally conceptualized in the theater, when the actors would turn to the audience and address them.

What to look for: a surprising moment when the narrator, protagonist, or a character speaks directly to you. You'll notice a shift in the pronouns used from he/she or I to "you". Often found when you read a quirky book, or have a very voicey narrator. Usually, the author will break the fourth wall early on in the story. Early as in the opening chapter. This is to prevent the reader being knocked out of the story because it's shocking later on.

Example

Are you listening? This is important. I want you, nay; I *need* you to focus on what I'm saying right now. You, dear reader, are experiencing a fourth wall break as I type.

Aside from Deadpool, *Fresh* by Margot Wood is a modern fiction example where the narrator and protagonist speak to you as the reader to bring you along on the journey.

What to break down

Fourth wall breaks are controversial. Some readers love it, others hate it. The reason for this is that most reading is about escapism, meaning the reader doesn't want to have the fact they're reading wafted in their face like a dead kipper. Alas, breaking the fourth wall does just that. It shoves a smelly, rotten fish carcass in your reader's face and obliterates the illusion of fantasy land. Characters aren't real. They can't and shouldn't be able to talk to the reader. That said, it's also seriously fun to fuck with the reader by creating a larger-than-life character. And that's exactly what this device does. So, what then, should you break down?

First, examine the level and depth of the fourth wall break. For example, in this nonfiction book, sometimes I refer to you, the reader, in reference to something you should or shouldn't be doing. This is a softer fourth wall break, one, because it's nonfiction, instructional and therefore the reader might expect a little talking to, and two because I am talking to you directly about this topic in a teacher-student manner. This is real life, kinda. But in fiction, the fourth wall breaks are much sharper because the reader won't expect to be spoken to like they might with nonfiction. How sharp, is something to examine. When the fourth wall break happens is also something to look at. In addition, why is the author doing it? What effect has it created? Is the break impactful in a good way or did it jar you out of the story and piss you off? What words or sentences were used to break the wall? How did it make you feel? Did it change the character's voice? Did the author format the break differently? At the sentence level how did it change the pace of the paragraphs or the tone and voice of the character? Does it make you feel closer to the character? Does it make the narrative read more like dialogue? If so, why? How? How does the narration change?

So. Many. Questions. And I literally just threw these off the top of my head. I'm sure you may have questions that are more relevant or perhaps more attuned to whatever you're trying to achieve in your own work. Bend and flex the questions to meet your needs.

∼

Tool: Personification

Personification occurs when an author gives human qualities to something that's not human. For example, the weather, animals, or objects.

What to look for: usually found in description. The author will pair a non-living thing with an action, emotion, or concept from a living entity.

Example

> "She waited, doubt tapping cold fingers on the back of her neck." Helen Glynn-Jones, *City of Wings and Gold*.

Like Victoria Lee's "guilt" earlier, doubt is also intangible, it is disembodied and not conscious, therefore can't have fingers. Doubt doesn't have fingers to tap necks. None of these things are true or real and yet, despite that, the personification of the emotion is simply exquisite. It creates a vivid picture of an insidious crawling hand over someone's neck.

What to break down

Oh, I do love a cheeky bit of personification. What object is the author personifying? Why that object? Is it important to the protagonist? Does it have meaning or symbolism? What is the comparison to? Is it compared to weather or an emotion? What imagery is being created by this comparison? Has it also been used in a different device, like a simile or metaphor? What about individual word choice? What would happen to the impact and effectiveness of the personification if the author had used different words? Why not switch a couple out and see how you feel about it as a sentence then? Is there any hidden meaning buried in the personification? Is it symbolic? Why did the character choose this "thing" to describe over anything else? Is the personification restricted to that one object? Is it a tool the author uses frequently throughout the story? Has an extended metaphor been employed?

So. Many. Questions. Guys, you gotta be curious. You gotta want to know shit about shit. For what it's worth, I wrote these questions before I even picked an example out for you. If you understand the basic concept of what a device is, you can start to come up with questions to break it down into its itty-bitty parts.

2.7 MID-LEVEL DECONSTRUCTION

What Counts as Mid-Level?

What constitutes mid-level story deconstruction?

For me, it's anything that's not so detailed that I'm deconstructing sentences, although sometimes we'll be looking for characterization at the sentence level because words create characters. But at mid-level, we're not looking at beautiful prose, description, or rhythm. We're looking at sentences to extract how character is made.

If we think about making a cake, the individual, separate ingredients are the sentence level. Once you combine them into a mushy paste mixture, it's the mid-level. Once baked in the oven, that's your macro-level analysis.

For me, I count anything character related. Characterization, character description, showing personality through narration, narrative voice—although of course, much of narrative voice comes from the sentence level, it's at this point I analyze voice specifically. Scenes, the pace, and the arc of a scene. The opening and closing hooks in a scene or chapter. I'd look at the location and placement of scenes. If the author has used unusual structures. For example, in V. E. Schwab's *Gallant*, there's a story within a story told through the perspective of the protagonist reading a journal. In the last book in my YA Fantasy trilogy, *Trey*, I used news bulletins between various chapters. I formatted the bulletins in a different font and they had a different tone too.

I might also look at the interplay of character relationships, such as the tension between hero and villain, the romance thread between protagonist and love interest. I might examine why a group of friends feels so exquisitely comforting.

Setting is another aspect I'd examine, both locations of scenes and the tone and atmosphere created—again here, the description and diving into the detail of why a description works blurs the line between micro-level and mid-level.

I also think of plot twists, but less in terms of story structure and more in a detailed way, such as what were the elements of the twist, and why did it work? What did the author set up or foreshadow or drop in as a red herring to make the twist work? As opposed to the positioning of the twist and how that fit into the story structure which I'd count as macro analysis—although for efficiency, I'd do it simultaneously rather than go away and come back to it later to look at it from the macro level.

Last, things like page-level analysis, I do here. You may feel like this is too high level for a mid-range element. But to me, each individual page is just that, a page. It's smaller than a scene, but comprised of multiple sentences. Ask yourself what does the author do with the page? Anything unusual with formatting, or perhaps with the amount of white space? I'm noticing more and more authors almost "copywriting" elements of their stories in order to mess with pacing, or speed up areas of their novels. Why? It hooks a reader and drags them through the story faster and faster.

What Does Mid-Level Deconstruction Look Like?

Let us begin with character. For me, I break character into two distinct sections: characterization and character arc.

Character is internal. It's the *who* of who a character is. It refers to the traits and whatever is at their core. Character is what you don't see, it's subtext and shadows, it's the foundations and pillars. And in deconstruction terms, that means their arc and the change they experience.

Characterization is everything on the surface. It's the physical appearance of your character. It's the clothes they wear, the tone of their dialogue, the observable actions in a story. It's what the reader sees and what shows them the "character" they can't see. In deconstruction terms, characterization covers everything from personality-driven actions to appearance, voice, habits, and dialogue and plot points. Character arc covers the change from a flawed state to a complete one at the end of the book.

Characterization Examples

What to Look For:

Appearance

I'm almost loathe to talk about a character's appearance, because the thing is, a reader is going to create a projection of what the character looks like in their head regardless of how we describe them. But authors who describe character well do it not by detailing pages of clothing and eye color, but by describing an aspect of their appearance that directly affects their personality or represents their personality. So, what do you look for? Any description of appearance that's unusual or brings into sharp relief an aspect of personality, like the librarian in the previous section, where Harrow describes the lipstick running into the cracks of the woman's lips. Look for characters that give you a crystal-clear image in your mind. When did that become so sharp? Usually, character descriptions are early in a story, or given to us the first time we meet a character.

Subtext

Subtext is everything not said, like when you disagree with your partner and they say, "I'm fine" and you know they are anything but fine. That is a glorious example of subtext. A character says one thing but means another. And of course, the art of this type of subtext comes from the setup, the precursors, or information you've given the reader to explain how the character really feels, so hunt for that too. But that's not the only example of subtext. You can see subtext through body language too.

Say the character you're reading about is speaking confidently through dialogue, but beneath the table, their hands are rubbing each other or shaking. This is subtext. It also tells you something about who the character really is. When a character says one thing but acts another way, this is a time to stop and figure out how the author has created that emotion and dissonance. When the character lies to themselves about what's going on and how they feel, this is another example of subtext.

Subtext is usually littered throughout a novel. But if it's specifically related to a character's growth, i.e., the dissonance is because they're lying to themselves, not yet confident or haven't overcome their flaw, then it will usually be prior to the dark night of the soul, and prior to arc completion.

Dialogue

Look for moments of dialogue where you feel you really hear the character's voice. Perhaps the character sounds different to other characters. Perhaps even before you read the tagline, you know who said it. Maybe the dialogue makes you laugh. There's no cut and dry you'll only find good dialogue "here". One hopes, it's all the way through a book.

Character Actions

In a novel, action is personality. Whatever your character does, defines who they are. But it's the actions that make a character stand out that you really want to pay attention to. For example, in the dystopian novel *Divergent* by Veronica Roth, everyone is grouped into "factions" where they live and work. Tris Prior is the protagonist and her parents expect her to be grouped into a humble faction called Abnegation. However, she actively chooses a different faction, Dauntless. But it's her actions that define her braveness throughout the story. For example, the Dauntless characters have to jump off a rooftop into a black hole you can't see the bottom of. Everyone is scared, and while they're deliberating who should go, Tris runs and jumps off the building, shutting everyone up. This action is her personality. It's the literal definition of dauntless and brave. Look for moments when characters stand out, or they shock you or they do something you don't expect, or something that goes against the grain. If you know a character is X (insert relevant personality trait or behavior) then look for the occasions they display X. Last, sometimes the context of what other characters are doing can provide a contrast that shines a light or augments the actions of another character. Take Spock and Captain Kirk from *Star Trek*. Their differences make their individual personalities even sharper and clearer. Which leads me to an example.

Example

""You're done?" I say as Dorian and I are still struggling to shove the guard in the closet.

"Please. Of course I'm done. These things are antiques. Even Dorian could hack them." Kato's eyes flick to Dorian and he gives him a wink." *Trey*, Sacha Black.

Here, the bit I want to focus on is the second line of dialogue. But this is an example where the pertinent line isn't enough alone. You need the context of the previous too.

Kato, is a full-blown, whip your titties out and shimmy with a feather boa type diva queen. He's also a bona fide genius, and he knows it, but while he can be a little arrogant, it's done in a cheeky diva-ish way, and usually he's helping someone. That's what this line shows.

The first line is the set up—the other two characters struggling. Kato is not. But rather than just saying "yes". He answers with sarcasm and banter and, to top off the banter, he slides Dorian a wink. His action of winking with the banter shows he's being playful rather than an arrogant twat. The reason I included both lines is that the contrast between Eden and Dorian's struggle enhances the clarity of Kato's achievement. It's also the setup for the banter to land.

Example

Let's do another example here. Characterization is endless with its options.

"As always, Donna had her fat arse plonked on one of the seats reserved for the old and frail. Built like a British Bulldog, top-heavy with a face that was meant for sniffing arseholes, Donna had her short stumpy legs propped up on a stool, her thick white ankles poked out from beneath her blue trousers." Scott Williamson, *Pearl's Tea, The Rebel Author Diaries.*

There is so much characterization in this line, where do I even start deconstructing it? First up, the length of the second sentence is long. This reflects the style of character. She's my all-time favorite grumbling, miserable old wench of a witch. And doesn't that extended, flowing description beautifully illustrate the way a grumpy witch might mumble under her breath?

Next up, this description works double for the author. Not only is it describing the character of Donna in rich imagery, but the *way* Donna is described tells you about the narrator (Pearl). Most characters do not compare faces to butt sniffing, they also wouldn't refer to someone's "fat arse". Not only is it an unexpected and subversive description, it tells you that Pearl is rebellious, doesn't have any fucks to give about anything, and says things exactly as they are. She's a character willing to push the line on all fronts. Williamson chose bold word choices that would intentionally shock. He extends the comparative metaphor of Donna's physical size to a breed of dog, by referencing her face to "sniffing butts" an action that dogs do regularly. If Pearl described Donna as having a scrunched-up face, it's a completely different image.

I thought this was an awesome device. I'm not sure I've seen an author compare a face to an action. But you could have all sorts of fun:

- She had a face like a sneeze.
- She had a face meant for drowning.
- She had a face like a hiccup.
- She had a face meant for suffocation.

On and on it goes.

There's still stacks more we could pull out of this. For example, in the latter half of the excerpt, Williamson uses a two-beat rhythm in his description.

"Donna had her [short stumpy] legs propped up on a stool, her [thick white] ankles poked out from beneath her blue trousers."

Arguably, there's two sets of two beats here in terms of adjective choice, short and stumpy, and then thick and white. These together give a flowing description. But they're also two insulting descriptives, which adds to how spiteful Pearl comes across. One insult wasn't enough of a descriptive for Pearl. She insulted Donna twice, or actually four times in one sentence. That tells you a lot about her. Character description. When you look at the rest of the first sentence, you can see the two-beat rhythm littered throughout the whole excerpt: British bulldog, fat arse, old, and frail.

What to break down

In my best Gollum voice, everything, my precious, everything. The core of characterization is action, so:

- What actions did the character do?
- What do those actions tell you about their personality?
- Why were those particular actions so powerful?
- Would you have chosen a different action?
- What would happen if you changed the action?
- Would it lessen or increase the characterization?
- Was there a set up?
- What word choice did the author use to describe the action that made it so distinctive?

- What was it about the tone or rhythm or specific word choice in the dialogue that made it so character like?
- How does the behavior/actions of the character you're observing affect the other characters around them?
- Or what are these other character's judgments and opinions of the original character?
- If you're breaking down subtext, what is the contrast or dissonance between what's said and what's meant or felt? Was there any set up to make this land?
- How far back was the groundwork laid?
- How many times was this foreshadowed?
- How is the author creating the subtext? Through body language clues, informing the reader of something the character doesn't know?
- How does POV impact the characterization?

Character Arc

The art of examining and deconstructing character arc is in the early observation. It's all about the shift from flawed to complete. To observe and deconstruct this, you need to establish the baseline character behavior and flaw—where they're coming from—to understand where they end up.

The easiest way to observe a character's flaws and desires is to look at the character's behavior.

What to Look For (if your character is a hero)

Bad, immoral or dubiously "gray" behaviors

Like stealing or lying (but usually for the right reason, like trying to protect or help their loved ones). Drinking, drugs, sleeping around, being moody or mean, intentionally isolating themselves.

Protagonists lying to themselves

This happens earlier in the story because the protagonist is in denial about their flaw and how they need to change. Characters lie to themselves about what they want or about what they need. They're usually in denial about their strengths or flaws, about another character or their feelings about that character. Sometimes they're in denial about something important or their actions and behaviors contradict their internal thoughts. This internal questioning of themselves and avoidance of certain subjects is a sure sign the protagonist will grow and change in this area.

The protagonist will see the truth of their lies during pivotal realization moments like the dark night of the soul or shortly after. For other side characters, you may not get to see their realization (depending on how major of a side character they are) and may only see their healed/complete selves towards the end of the book.

Judgment from other characters

Later in the character arc, the protagonist's friend will get sick of their flawed behavior. But being the dutiful friends they are, they'll attempt to bestow their judgment on the hero to help them see the light. This happens somewhere between the midpoint up to the dark night of the soul.

Think bromance moments where the BFF (or mentor, parent, significant other character) calls out the protagonist for their shitty behavior, which inevitably the protagonist denies because they're not quite at arc completion yet. Like *Mean Girls*, when Janis calls out Cady's behavior because she's being thoughtless and behaving like the school bitch, Regina.

Poor choices and decision making

This is the aspect of protagonists I, personally, find the most frustrating when reading or viewing. I have eyeball twitching moments where I want to scream at the page or the TV and say "Really? WHY, Anthony, WHYYYYY??" and yes, for lovers of *Bridgerton*, that was a reference to the tantalizing enemies to lovers romance in season two.

Protagonists make poor decisions earlier in the story. The decisions should connect to the protagonist's flaw too. What is it the character needs to learn? Whatever that is, then that's the type of situations the character should decide on.

For example, if the character needs to learn to trust others, then they should be put in situations where they have to trust others. But, still being flawed, they struggle to trust and thus make poor decisions. Their poor decision *is* the lack of trust in others.

But what do you look for?

Clearly a choice-making situation. But if that is hard to find, then the easiest thing to spot is when something goes wrong for the protagonist. Track back to the decision they made that led to their current situation and the consequences they're facing. What was the setup? What wound made it hard to trust?

Moments of change

This is perhaps the most critical of all the observations to make. Unlike side characters, the protagonist's arc should require the entire novel to complete. Therefore, it is the slow shifting from one state to another that is the foundation of a solid arc, not a whiplash change. This means there will be small or subtle clues to look out for.

- A change in stance or view on a particular subject where they had an ardent viewpoint.
- A shift in body language despite the words they're saying.
- A move towards spending time with a new character.
- A change in the way they're talking or the things that are important to them.

A character forms through his, her or their hero lens. A concept I talk more about in *10 Steps to Hero: How to Craft a Kickass Protagonist*. Essentially, the hero lens comprises four parts: thoughts, feelings, actions, and dialogue. These four embody a character. When a character expresses any of these, it's an opportunity to deconstruct or examine to see if there is a change or shift away from their flawed personality.

There are other key moments of change in a novel too. Plot points, turning points, dark night of the soul, the inciting incident. These are all locations where pivotal scenes will occur, where the protagonist will face a choice and therefore there will be consequences. Something ends and something begins. Stop and deconstruct or examine what the author has done and how each of these plot points connects.

The start and end of anything is usually fraught with emotion too. Examine how the author has made the scene emotional.

- Is there more description?
- Are there more sensory details?
- Is there more introspection than in other areas of the scene?

- Does the protagonist realize something?
- What prompted the realization?
- How does the author depict the change in the character?
- Of the four elements of the hero lens, what changes and what stays the same?

Example

In book three of my YA fantasy series, the Eden East novels, the protagonist Eden is suffering with grief from the loss of loved ones. Over the early part of the story, she becomes an addict to an illegal and very potent form of magical pain relief, and as a result, she makes poor choices in order to continue receiving the pain relief. Some obstacles she faces are in direct consequence to that. One moment occurs when she's outed on national TV and her addiction is on display for the entire world to see. But this is also the driver that pushes her towards changing. It's both conflict and also signals the end of her old cycle of flawed behavior.

What to Break Down

- How self-aware is the protagonist about their flaw and how is that shown?
- What blockages, obstacles, or areas of conflict does the protagonist encounter that are directly caused by their flaw?
- How are their behaviors and choices different at the end of the book compared to the start of the book?
- Do they get a do over? By that I mean a scene where the protagonist faces a similar decision as they did at the beginning of the book, but they know to make the opposite choice this time.

- Do they make up for their poor actions?

Character Arcs in Side Characters

For a comprehensive look at character arcs in side characters, I recommend reading my book on these little munchkins, *8 Steps to Side Characters: How to Craft Supporting Roles with Intention, Purpose, and Power*. Not every side character will have an arc for so many reasons I detail in that book. But let's say there's a character you want to deconstruct, and they have an arc. What are you looking for?

The character with the deepest arc and most amount of page time devoted to it will be the protagonist. So your side characters will only be able to detail parts of their arc. Usually, the before flawed state and the after resolution. If they're a major side character, they may have a moment or two related to a subplot where they show their struggle but not to the depth of the protagonist.

Setting

Let's move away from characters and look at setting as a mid-level point of deconstruction. Setting is a dark horse. It's the unloved stepchild. But holy crap, can you do some amazing things when you engage setting as a tool in your story.

What to Look For: often the bulk of setting description comes when a character moves to a new location. Or when they're interacting with an element of the setting. This is because a good story will ground the reader in time, place, and point of view. So the start of every new chapter and scene is an opportunity to do just that. Hunt for setting clues early on in chapters, or after a locational transition. Another time you find setting is in the lead up to an emotional moment in the story as it helps to provide atmosphere. Are there moments when you feel like you have a vivid image of the environment? Perhaps the weather is going gangbusters, does the location the character is in give you the heebie-jeebies?

Example

> "Far below the darkest waters, in a cell made of bones, a creature was born. She was the only one of her kind to have entered the realm in such a way: on the cold, bloody stones of Saddoriel's prison." *A Lair of Bones,* Helen Scheuerer.

This is the opening line in the prologue of Helen Scheuerer's epic fantasy novel *A Lair of Bones.* Even as the story opens, Scheuerer is drawing the reader in with exquisite descriptions of the setting. Clearly, the setting is important to the story. This *is* the lair of bones the title refers to. The description is rich in imagery. There's more to this example, but we'll examine that detail in a moment. Key descriptive words here that lay the setting are "darkest waters" "cell made of bones" "realm" and then the final clause in its entirety "cold, bloody stones of Saddoriel's prison."

The setting here is so rich because of the specific word choice. Instead of Scheuerer slapping out "*below* the waters," it's *far* below, and the waters aren't just water. They're the *darkest.*

Augmenting your description and setting is often about leveling up your word choice, making it sharper, more acute. Don't be a slut for casual wordery. Be picky, go for Michelin starred words instead of the local pub burger.

Instead of walking, choose saunter. Instead of eating, choose inhale. Likewise, a prison cell is descriptive by itself. We all know what a prison looks like. But this prison is different, and it's the difference Scheuerer cleverly described. Instead of metal bars, the prison is made of bones. Umm what? How effing creepy is that? No good shit comes from being encased in a bone prison. Let me tell you, sunshine.

And last, realm is indicative of the fact we're entering a fantasy world. Interestingly, this sentence also cleverly introduces not one, but three characters from the off. The creature born, and therefore by default, there must be a "birther/mother" of the creature and Saddoriel. So. Much. Information. In just one sentence.

What to break down

- What is the composition of the environment?
- How does this differ from what's expected?
- If the location is grounded in reality, how much detail has the author used to create a comprehensive setting?
- What elements did the author or character choose to describe?
- And what does this tell you about what the character values or deems important?
- What objects has the author highlighted? For example, if it's a war field, are there tanks?
- What weapons are described?
- What is the emotion in the setting and how does it connect?
- Does the setting impact the characters? If so, how?
- What sensory experiences do you have as a reader? For example, in a war scene, as well as the visual horror, there would be sounds of explosions, intense physical pain from injuries, perhaps the matted smells of mud and the metallic tang of iron.
- How does the author use the senses to enrich the setting?
- Which senses are favored?

- What elements of description make the setting come alive?
- How does the character interact with the setting?
- Do they comment, interact with, or only observe the setting?
- How does this level of interaction change the depth of imagery?

Scene and Chapter Deconstruction

Start and End Hooks

Examine the first and last sentence first. Then the first and last paragraphs. This is where the author should lay the groundwork to hook you into the next scene.

What to Look for

Well, awks, but there's only one place to go for this information. The start and end of "things". I say things because there are many starts and ends in books. Not just the opening and closing sentence—although these are the obvious place to start. But in every novel, there is more than one storyline. There's usually at least a B plot and sometimes a C and D plot.

Typically, a new character brings new story threads, new information, new emotions, or complications. Look for when a plan changes in the plot or when characters veer in a new direction.

There's another obvious point here: you find the "starts" and "hooks" earlier in stories. By the midpoint, it's unusual to have too many new subplots or characters. The exception to that rule is when you're writing in a series and you want to foreshadow and lay the groundwork for a hook into the next book. And, of course, lest we forget the start and end of each chapter, and the need for hooks at both points to continue drawing the reader through and creating that page turning I'm-so-screwed-for-work-I'm-staying-up-until-three-a.m. feel.

Conversely, endings come in the second half of the book. In order for something to be ended, it needs to have happened and been processed by the characters. You need page time and plot for that. The exception is when you're in a series and a thread spills over from a previous book. Rounding it off or concluding it early in the plot of a later (in the series) book might make sense.

Look for highly emotive scenes. Often these emotional outcomes and reactions are at the end point of a subplot, or, if a romantic or relationship subplot, then they occur just before the conclusion.

Cliffhangers also count in this section.

Example

Back to Ms. Scheuerer's excellent prologue opener.

"Far below the darkest waters, in a cell made of bones, a creature was born. She was the only one of her kind to have entered the realm in such a way: on the cold, bloody stones of Saddoriel's prison." *A Lair of Bones,* Helen Scheuerer.

There are other reasons this opening gambit is so good. It's also using foreshadowing. The sentence refers to a unique creature, "the only one" when something is special or unique in a book, there's usually a reason. The reader knows this innately, which is why this is an excellent hook. Readers want to know why that character is the only one, why *them?* It raises questions, and questions have to be answered. It's like wafting catnip under a kitty's nostrils.

Kitty gotta have the nip-nip.

Scheuerer's sentence is both exquisitely descriptive and purposely vague. The vagueness comes from not naming or identifying the character in the sentence. Sentences have subjects until they don't on purpose. It's clear this is an intentionally devious usage of not naming someone. It also tells the reader something. That this character will be important later in the story. That's something the reader will pay attention to. Not having a name or an identifier gives the reader a reason to read on, a mystery to unravel, and a question to solve later in the book. How will the characters in the prison cell connect to the plot? Will they escape? Why are they in the cell in the first place and why did a pregnant person get imprisoned? So. Many. Questions. And all from just one clever sentence.

What to Break Down

- Where is the start or end located?
- Is it the literal and physical start and end of a book?
- Is it the start and end of a chapter or scene?
- Where is the scene located and what does that tell you about the plots or subplots?
- Who is driving the end of the plot?
- What is the emotional tension at the start or end point?
- Does the author use sensory writing to heighten the emotion and tension?
- How does it make you feel?
- Is the resolution satisfying? If so, why? Was it inevitable? If the answer is yes, then you should track back through the book to find where the hints of the ending were seeded, because I assure you, they were. If an ending is satisfying, it's because the author is a crafty bastard and made it so.

- What if a chapter contains many scenes? How does each scene in the chapter start and end? Are the scenes connected to each other?
- Does time run linearly or jump about with the shifting scenes?
- Does the author make you skip to a different POV to keep you turning the pages because you simply have to get back to that last POV?
- What is the start or end of the scene, chapter, or subplot made of? Was it dialogue, narration, action, a question, a revelation, a death?
- Where do these subplots start? Are they at highly tense points? Usually subplots are put in place to push the protagonist towards or away from whatever their arc needs to be, so is this subplot a driver or a distraction?
- How does it connect to the theme?

Cliffhangers, although they're the marmite-love-hate ending for readers, have their place. The first thing to assess is how hard of a cliffhanger it is. Hard cliffhangers are a little more dangerous. They leave major plot threads incomplete. This can be like poking a burning beehive. Softer cliffhangers are usually related to subplots, or the opening of a new subplot that will lead into the next book.

Another example here would be the end of my first book, *Keepers*. While I won't spoil the ending, the main thread and storyline is resolved. But the B plot is a bubbling rivalry. There's a character that "appears" to be dead and then returns to cause trouble right at the end of the first book. The story ends with a gasp but is still satisfying to the reader because the main will-they-won't-they romance line is resolved.

Questions to ask about cliffhangers include the impact the

cliffhanger has on the reader's satisfaction with the overall story.

- Did it make them (or you if you're the reader) want to read on?
- Or did it just piss you off?
- Was it an A-plot or B-plot cliffhanger?
- What was the cliffhanger? A question? A character? A threat?
- How well was the cliffhanger foreshadowed or seeded earlier in the book?

2.8 MACRO-LEVEL DECONSTRUCTION

Macro-Level Observations

And now we reach macro-level analysis. And what, exactly is macro deconstruction? I like to think of this as a wide-angle lens. You know those ridiculous fishy-faced, boggle lenses that make your eyes look like gob stoppers? That, but for story.

Here we examine the structure of story itself. We study the culmination of things we found that made the book more than just the ink smears on the page.

For me, macro-level observations include:

- Genre, pacing and plot
- Tone and atmosphere
- Theme and symbolism

Genre, Pacing and Plot

These three are tricky to analyze. There isn't one sentence you can deconstruct to give you a definitive. This is more about pulling back and examining the whole feel and shape of the story. How does it hang together in your mind? Sure, individual lines or hooks or playing with punctuation can speed up prose, but this is about the overall story.

When I examine genre, I want to understand and compare the overarching story to that of others in the genre. How is it similar? How is it different? Overarching pacing covers how fast or slow the book is. Where does the author intentionally play with pacing? If structure is important to the genre, i.e., most romances follow a very similar beat sheet, I'd examine how the romance adhered to or veered away from that structure. If it was a thriller, I'd look at how the author wove elements of mystery through the novel. Where were the clues placed? What were the red herrings and when and where were they employed?

How is the story told? First person POV, third? Is it told in the past tense or present? Does it employ a "then and now" structure flipping between periods in time and history? What are the subplots and how do they link to, and influence, the main plot? Where do characters part and reunite if it's an epic quest story?

Is the author using a trope? How do they either stick to the known or desired elements of the trope and how do they twist it up to make it new and fresh? How does the twist affect the story? Is it a retelling? If so, how does the story match the original? How is it different? What element was used to turn the retelling on its head?

Structure wise, I might go back and purposefully find the inciting incident or the midpoint and ferret around those couple of pages to see how and where the author has placed them in the story and whether they work as their story structure element. Was the inciting incident impactful enough? Was it believable? Would you have been able to turn away from the challenge?

What to Look For

If you're keen to deconstruct a winning plot, look for the key scenes in the story, the pivotal moments of change or obstacles. Where do the highly charged scenes occur? Where is the hero facing a problem? Where is there a tragic or joyous occurrence? Where is your heart pounding? Key scenes I hunt for include: the inciting incident or the moment the hero gets dragged into the story, any plot twists that occur, the midpoint, the dark night of the soul, the climax, and resolution. Most of the rest of the plot points are usually variations of push pull as the protagonist struggles with their flaw and the obstacles connected to it.

Example

In 2.7, I mentioned the last book in my YA fantasy series, *Trey*. I referenced a scene where Eden is outed for her controversial addiction to pain relief on national TV. A false low (as the book has an HEA, of sorts). The incident pushes her to take control of her situation and get a grip. It's the point where there's a noticeable shift in her behavior. She drives the plot in the direction she wants it to go rather than letting things happen to her. Sounds like a midpoint change in story structure terms. Guess where that event occurs in the book... The literal midpoint, the end of the seventeenth of thirty-four chapters.

What to Deconstruct

It depends in part on what plot point or part of story structure you're examining. But if we take the midpoint above, you would need to know whether it was a false high or false low. What was the event or obstacle that pushed the hero into action? What were the emotions in the scene? You could go granular here and deconstruct the sensory elements, the body language, and the tools in descriptions.

Other things to deconstruct include the change or shift that happens. In major plot points, the story always pivots or takes a turn. What is the new direction? How does that impact the tone and pace of the story?

You need to know the purpose of the plot point in order to deconstruct it. Like deconstructing the inciting incident to see how the author drags the hero into the story. Or deconstructing the dark night of the soul to understand emotional lows and revelations.

Examine the pace in the most pivotal moments. Is the race up to the pivotal scene fast but the actual scene itself slow? Or is it the opposite? What changes the pace? Is it the level of emotion and introspection the character does? Is it the sentence construction? Shorter sentences speed up the pace. Less description creates more pace, the more description there is, the slower the story gets. How do side characters react in those pivotal scenes? How do the relationships change between them and the protagonist?

Tone and Atmosphere

For me, tone is about the general feel of your story. Is it funny? A parody or satirical? Is it dark and chilling? Or perhaps the tone is more coming of age and about growth and hope. Again, a hard one to capture, but something to look at as-a-whole once you've read the book. There will be sentences and examples you can point to in the books that will reflect tone, but mostly it's the cumulative effect that creates the tone. Repeated instances of humor, repeated instances of chilling descriptions.

Atmosphere, though, is variable and changes throughout

the book depending on the emotional tension, the action, and drama in each scene and what plot is happening.

Tone

Book one in my YA series is light and fun. While there are dark twists and turns, the overall feel is one of friendship and hope and finding your soul mate. By the time you get to the third book, the tone is completely different. It's much darker and grittier. If I were analyzing the books, I'd deconstruct things like:

The emotional differences: book one is all about first love and friendship. Book three is about loss, grief and finding the strength to defeat the big villain.

Narrative difference

Book 1:

"I can't dance. Like, really can't dance. This isn't one of those left feet, bad dad-dancing things either. There is something wrong with my DNA. Put me in a training ring, and I'll fight like a tornado. But put me on a dance floor, and my body ceases to function, let alone obey ballroom commands."

The protagonist worries about a lot of shallow and surface level issues like what they're wearing to balls or gossip. But by the time you get to the last book, her entire world has changed. Surface things don't matter and they're all experiencing loss and grief and what matters is holding on to each other. In the above example, the references are light like "dad-dancing". The example below is much darker, full of descriptive words for pain instead of fun. Word choices like gloom, darkness, violence, sharp, and panic all help to shift the tone over the course of the book.

Book 3:

"The darkness is violent.

For a while, there's nothing. The gloom slithers around me, a mass of writhing eels. It thickens to a pulp and coats my thoughts.

I'm drowning. Sharp noises. Cuts of panic.

Where fingers touch my skin, it burns like the kiss of a branding iron.

Something rips. My insides pull apart.

Pieces of me sear and spit fire like solar flares. I reach for the molten torture, but it shifts and moves."

Atmosphere

Atmosphere is easier to spot in terms of its creation, as there is usually a sentence or cluster of sentences that will create the atmosphere within a scene. As it can shift and change from scene to scene, it's easier to spot than tone.

Let's look at a couple of examples.

"Hayden saw them in the white, visions of his parents, the pair of them screaming until their voices were hoarse. His mother slapping his father, his father belting his mother. Dog yapping at their feet. His father taking a boot to Dog's head. Dog didn't last long after that. Mom said she forgave his father eventually, but her eyes told different. Eyes can't lie like mouths can." Daniel Willcocks, *When Winter Comes*.

Cowers under a pillow

I've started with this because it's freaking terrifying and it's a little different. It's not a direct or obvious example of atmosphere setting. Most of the time, you'd expect an example of atmosphere to be describing the temperature or "feeling" of a room or environment, perhaps the weather or other external factors. And those are all excellent ways to create atmosphere. But this is an interesting example because it doesn't do that and creates atmosphere, anyway.

First up, the character, Hayden, is seeing things, "visions". This automatically makes the reader uneasy. It makes the character vulnerable, which raises the tension. Willcocks uses chilling and violent descriptive words and actions like screaming, hoarse and slapping. There's violence bubbling under the description, again adding tension to the atmosphere.

There's another quirky use of voice in this quote, Willcocks uses "dog" only. Not "the dog" but simply, dog. Willcocks, the dark devil, has created something grammatically subversive. For the reader, it's jarring in the best way possible. The friction in the rhythm of the sentence reflects the uneasy atmosphere. There's another trick used here in the way the character describes what's happening. The dog dies, but instead of grieving and expressing sadness, the dog dying is described almost as a throwaway sentence. Now that is terrifying! Willcocks also uses a yin-yang cadence with this sentence "His mother slapping his father, his father belting his mother." So much violence laced through, and yet, both clauses have five words. The violence flows from mother to father and back again. But that makes this easy written and flowing prose juxtapose against the actual violent content. And that last sentence? *Chef's kiss*.

Example

Let's look at another example. This one is from Helen Glynn Jones, *Light and Dark*, Volume 5 of the Ambeth Chronicles.

"He was well and truly sober now. Adrenaline and his stone sharpened every edge, every noise, every shadow. The Hunt assembled, their fierce hawk-like faces above blackened armour, red jewels glinting like blood as their horses pranced and snorted, tossing their manes... Feathered purple clouds streaked the sky, the first stars peeping through. It was time to ride."

This is a sumptuous example of atmospheric writing. We're straight in with a "sobering" line, bringing the atmosphere back from wherever it was (I'm assuming drunk fun and frolics) to serious. There's a lyrical beat, beat, beat to the end of the second sentence. Jones uses punctuation and the intentional repetition of "every" to draw attention to the more tense and chilling aspects around the character. It layers up those elements by banging them out one after the other. She's also made careful word choices like fierce, blackened, and blood to create a more ominous feeling. Darker words = darker atmosphere. Last, the horses' actions are impatient and that adds to the atmosphere, creating a tense, anticipatory feel.

Theme and Symbolism

Thematic elements and symbolism are some of my favorite elements to hunt for. They're subtle and clever and usually the author is a devious little monkey with how they weave them in. What is the theme of the story? How and where does this theme show up in the book? How have they woven that into the story at macro-, micro-, and mid-levels? When looking at theme stated in a line of prose, it can blur the line between all three levels of analysis. That's even more so the case when examining symbolism.

Symbolism can and probably should weave through all three levels. There is the overall symbolism in a book connected to the theme and meaning of the story. But characters themselves can be symbolic, they can do and say things that have symbolic meaning, and of course, you can drench your sentence level prose in meaning and symbols, too.

This is perhaps the hardest section to give tangible examples without plonking an entire book inside this chapter and pointing out all the pieces.

Symbolism is simply when one element represents another. For example, when the weather represents the mood of the scene, like when a storm happens as the tension grows or something bad is about to happen. Another example is a metaphor for rage that includes references to fire, lava, or heat. All symbolic of the sensations of rage. But it could be an object, lyric, or song.

You can find symbolism in the tiniest of details in setting and prose all the way through to large-scale scenes that are symbolic in and of themselves.

Theme then, is the golden thread the author expertly stitches through the novel. It's the real meaning of the story. It's not the plot. In *The Hunger Games,* the plot is a battle to the death for loads of kids on reality TV. The theme is deeper than that. It's the message and the meaning beneath the text. In *The Hunger Games* that would be sacrifice. Theme is usually an abstract concept, something philosophically deep and meaningful.

What to Look For: Theme

Some stories (especially Disney movies) will state the theme explicitly. In fact, for theme spotting, it's a great idea to start with Disney movies because their films are based around a theme or moralistic lesson they want to teach kids. Usually, a side character will state the theme early on when the protagonist is still flawed and, of course, the protagonist completely ignores the lesson. Right up, that is, until they complete their arc and the theme gets restated as a lesson learned and action the protagonist takes.

Example

In the Disney movie *Planes*, the side character Franz states the theme.

"...thanks from all of us that want to do more than what we were just built for." Franz, *Planes*.

Dusty is a crop spraying plane, but he wants to be more than that. He wants to be a racer plane, but when the story starts, he doesn't believe he can be.

In books, there's often a moment where a side character, friend, or mentor might question the protagonist about something they're doing. Of course, this won't always happen and sometimes the theme is less explicit, there you need to keep digging.

Examine the enormous obstacles the protagonist is facing. What is the protagonist's fundamental flaw? When hunting for the theme, examine the main choice the protagonist has to make. Or perhaps look at the aspect of themselves they need to give up in order to win. Last, the choice they have to make which is usually between two terrible options. Another way to hunt for the theme is to examine the beginning of a book. What's the hook or the promise of the story? It should connect to the theme and therefore that's one puzzle piece to help you extrapolate out the theme.

What to Deconstruct

How easy was it for you to put your finger on what the

theme was? While it might be hard to pin into a singular word or sentence, it should be fairly obvious. How is the theme woven into the story? Is it woven in at multiple layers? For example, are there sentence level references to the theme? Actions the protagonist takes, obstacles the protagonist has to overcome that directly link to the theme? Are there conversations or revelations around the theme? How subtle is the theme? Is it on the nose like Disney? Or harder to spot? Is the theme concluded or does the author leave it to the reader to make their own mind up?

What to Look For: Symbolism

An item or element that means something to the protagonist or character. Something that holds value, be it emotionally, physically, financially or because of family or any other reason. Or an item that recurs or is in the background. The subtler the symbolism, the harder it is for the reader to identify. I always feel clever if I identify symbolism and I find myself rather taken with authors that make me feel clever.

Example

In *Under the Whispering Door* by T. J. Klune, there's a ghost dog that is adorable and lovely. The grumpy protagonist doesn't get on with anyone at the start of the book, but as he pushes through his character arc, his relationship with the dog changes. The better their relationship is, the closer he gets to completing his character arc. So the relationship with the dog is symbolic of his arc change. There are other elements of symbolism in the story too. For example, the protagonist wears stiff suits while alive, symbolizing his cold, pole-up-his-ass personality. But as the book progresses, he's forced into softer, more casual clothes like pajamas and flip-flops and all manner of things that are the antithesis of what he used to be. But they're also more symbolic of his new changing state. Another example is the balloons in the movie *Up,* which represent hopes and dreams. In *Lord of the Flies* by William Golding, the conch is a symbol of authority and leadership.

What to Deconstruct

What detail or item did the author choose to be symbolic? How does that connect to the theme or deeper meaning in the story? Why is the symbol significant to the protagonist and where was that laced earlier in the story? Was it mentioned in backstory? Was it referred to by another character? How and at what point in the story were you first made aware of the symbol? How does the symbol make the protagonist feel? What visceral or emotional responses does the protagonist have? Are the senses engaged at the sentence and descriptive level? What colors and imagery are used in connection with the symbol?

Motif

What is a motif? A motif is a form of symbolism. It's symbolic in its nature, but it's also different in that it's a recurring or repetitive element. For example, in *The Hunger Games*, the Mockingjay bird is a motif. There's a hand symbol representative of the Mockingjay that the characters perform. There's a song often sung that represents the Mockingjay birdsong. Katniss wears the symbol of the Mockingjay throughout the story too. It represents everything Katniss's people stand for, which is why it's repeated in so many ways throughout the book. A motif is usually a concrete "thing" unlike theme, which is more abstract.

What to Look For

Anything that repeats. Does a physical item get mentioned or shown on page multiple times? Is there a repeated location in the book? Is there a badge or symbol seen frequently? Perhaps there's a flower that's used multiple times.

Example

We've already mentioned the Mockingjay from *The Hunger Games*. But the yellow brick road in *The Wizard of Oz* is another motif. It appears multiple times through the story, is the literal path they follow to reach their destination and even has a song attached to it.

What to Deconstruct

How and when is the motif first introduced? What is its meaning? How often is it used? Is the motif connected to the theme? Is the motif important to one character or many? Is there a second layer or meaning connected to the motif? Is the motif used in different ways? I.e., as a symbol, the song, and the hand gesture in *The Hunger Games*.

Structure Games

How is structure different to plot? Here I mean the literal and physical structure of the book. Plot is the structure of the story. But here, I am referring to things like the Point of View, whether it's told in a shifting timeline, or if there are multiple POVs. Is there a story within a story? I'd deconstruct what that looked like, how it weaves into the story and what clever tricks the author uses to pull it off. Does the author use text messages, emails, or journal entries? How does the tone of voice and style of voice or formality change in those elements compared to normal narrative prose? Does the author use quotes at the top of their work? Is the story told linearly or not?

What to Look For

The physical nature of the book. How do the chapters start? Is it with a quote or something other than pure narration? Is the story told in a linear chronological order or is it told in bits and pieces and in a structure that's flip flopping? Is there one timeline or many? How are flashbacks used?

Example

The Time Traveler's Wife by Audrey Niffenegger is told in a non-linear order, as is *Vicious* by V. E. Schwab. Both jump backwards and forwards in time while still telling a coherent story. Lauren Oliver's *Delirium* has quotes above each chapter, as do my YA fantasy books and some of my nonfiction. For example, one of the quotes in *Trey* is:

'We are the makers of our own fate.'
The new Laws of Trutinor

I use the quotes to deliver little added snippets of world building information, insights into laws, journal entries, newspaper reports, and other information that isn't in the major thrust of the story but adds a little more depth to the world. I use those quotes for another sneaky reason, too. Often, if you pay attention, they're foreshadowing things to come.

What to Deconstruct

It depends what element of structure you have found. If it's an unusual timeline like *The Time Traveler's Wife*, what does that do to the reader's understanding? Does the story still flow in a satisfying way? What seeds are sowed earlier in the book in strange time periods to pull the ending off?

If the author uses quotes at the top of the chapters, like I use at the top of each new step, what do they do? Do they foreshadow? Give world building tidbits or are they symbolic somehow? How do these structural elements interact with the story and plot line or characters? If it's a story within a story, how do the stories connect? How do they affect each other? Is there any crossover? Are they on the same timeline? What would happen if you changed the order of the story? Are the elements written in the same tone and voice as the rest of the story? If not, why not? If you're deconstructing a flashback, how does it connect to the real time story? How does the incident in the flashback impact the protagonist? How does it change his, her, or their behavior?

Example

The Hazel Wood by Melissa Albert has elements of fairytale stories woven into her plot. The fairytale stories are native to her fantasy world, like fantasy mythology. Parts of the fairytales are told during the main plot, but they have a slightly different tone and voice to the main narration. And in fact, she bundled them up (wrote more) and put them into an anthology as an addition to the series, a great marketing tactic. Lauren Oliver, author of the *Delirium* series, used quotes at the top of her chapters. These quotes came from her world's fictional bible called "The Book of Shh". Like Albert, she bundled them up and padded out the book to create a real *Book of Shh* and published it as a series add-on.

Foreshadowing

Foreshadowing happens when the author shows or indicates something will happen before it actually does. Usually in very subtle ways.

What to Look For

Breadcrumbs. Usually foreshadowing happens with tiny breadcrumb drops the reader isn't necessarily supposed to pick up on.

Foreshadowing is at its best when it's shown and not told. Look for items you're shown as the reader. Perhaps the protagonist is told (or states) something in black and white terms—a sure sign that neither of those things will come to bear. What's missing is often as much of a clue as what's shown. Unspoken words, snide comments, questions that are difficult for the protagonist to answer, big events on the horizon foreshadow trouble to come. Occasions where you're shown something and then the attention is diverted away immediately after. That's a sign of intentional misdirection, too. Warnings, look out for those. Like when mom says to her kid, just don't leave the house, don't go in the garage and the kid is all "Sure, mom." And then *they* do exactly that. You know shit is about to go down.

Example

In the James Bond movie *Spectre,* the film starts at the Day of the Dead (Día de Muertos) festival, a literal nod to the fact the villain ends up being a character Bond thought was dead. Not only that, but the name of the movie is symbolic, Spectre. Another word for ghost—a nod to what's coming. These are just two of the elements in the opening scene, but even as early as the title of the movie, the film is foreshadowing the ending.

It's these elements that give readers or viewers that inevitability feeling. That sense of "I knew it" or deep sighing satisfaction.

What to Deconstruct

First, examine how many breadcrumbs are dropped and how obvious they are to find. Foreshadowing is often easier to find on the second read through because you know what the story is and therefore can spot clues to the ending that were hidden the first time through.

Where do the clues get laced in?

- At what point in the story and how often are they foreshadowed?
- Are the clues people or object related?
- Is it a feeling you get or a clear line in the story that gives it away?
- If the foreshadowing is laced into the description, how did the author weave the clue in?
- What literary device did they use?
- What word choice did they make that showed you the omen without overtly stating it?
- Do the clues relate to each other, or are they foreshadowing different events?
- How long of a page and time gap is there between the clue being dropped and the payoff? Sometimes it can feel cliched or obvious if the clue and payoff are too close together. Likewise, if they're too far apart, the impact is lost because the reader forgot.
- Last, did the author use subtext to aid in the foreshadowing?

2.9 THE FIRST AND LAST PAGE

Spoiler Warning: *A Lair of Bones* by Helen Scheuerer (the opening page), *Killing Eve,* the final season and last episode specifically. *Keepers* by Sacha Black, *Sweet and Bitter Magic* by Adrienne Tooley.

Whether or not you want to hear this, the first page contains the most important words inside your book for hooking your reader into your story and onto the next page... and then onto the next and the next. See, once the reader is hooked, if you're clever and sprinkle just the right amount of questions, delightful characters, and intriguing subplot fuckery, your readers will continue through your story like the heavily drugged book hippies they are. But you have to hook them first. This is why I make a point of heavily deconstructing the first page of each best seller I read.

What Can You Get from the First Page?

We all know the first page is important, but I wonder how much attention you really give it? The first page, along with the first couple of chapters, is foundational for any book. When we approach the first page and chapters as a writer, we know we have to establish:

- The protagonist's "before" world.
- Their flaw and want.
- Allude to the theme.
- Hint at the villain or inner conflict.
- We have to introduce one or two other key characters.
- Make sure our narrative voice is crisp.
- Make sure the character voices are crisp.
- Establish the setting.
- Some level of world building.
- Create a hooky first line.
- Tone of the book.

It's a helluva lot. But *gestures at the first page* it's also why paying attention to page one and the full first chapter is crucial. If the above list is what we focus on when writing, then it's what we should focus on when deconstructing a best seller, too.

Start with the First Sentence

I'm a bit of a slut when it comes to first lines. I collect them. Stuff 'em into jars and notebooks taxidermy style so I can keep them forever.

I'm becoming more and more convinced that my favorite first lines, the ones that really have lasting impact, are the ones that a) have a purpose and b) are copy written. The books that really grab my attention are the ones whose first lines slam into me like a giant dil... dilapidated ocean liner. In the next chapter, we'll dive into some examples of first lines and how they make them pop.

Sometimes the true meaning of a first line isn't apparent until you've finished the book. Look for techniques like:

- Mirroring: check the first and last lines to see if they're mirrors of each other (which also reflects the change in the protagonist and the completion of their arc).
- A statement saying something controversial or unexpected about the protagonist or a controversial opinion the protagonist holds.
- A juxtaposition or contradiction.
- Personification.
- A problem posed.
- Foreshadowing (you may only realize this once you've read the book).
- A question, a promise, a hook.

These are some of the tools I've pulled out of the books I've read, but the possibilities are endless. Let's go a bit deeper.

Captain Hook

Hooks draw a reader into the story. They dig into a reader's heart and yank them through the story like the flappy book-fish they are.

Always check the first page for hooks. I like to think of hooks and promises as anything that make you raise a penciled brow and want to read on. Like tension filtering in, questions raised, half-information, half-truths, scraps of unfinished details. It's all delicious and teases the reader. But what does that look like in practice?

Let's examine Helen Scheuerer's opening page of *A Lair of Bones* because it has an impressive number of promises and hooks. First, the excerpt without any commentary:

"Far below the darkest waters, in a cell made of bones, a creature was born. She was the only one of her kind to have entered the realm in such a way: on the cold, bloody stones of Saddoriel's prison. In the waning torchlight, her mother, the prisoner, closed her lilac eyes. Bracing herself against the raw beat of lingering pain, she already sensed the death song that hummed within her daughter, as strong as the ancestors before her. It was the quiet promise of poignant keys and mesmerizing notes: magic. Ready to be honed into one of the most powerful weapons known to the realms above, belonging to a cyren of the vast and ancient deep. The prisoner gazed down at the small being in the crook of her elbow. In all her centuries of existence, she had never seen a newborn up close before, and this one was *hers*. She peered at the tiny, pink face in wonder. Without the glimmer of scales at her temples, or the dark fingernails that turned to talons, the infant could have been human."

I don't know about you, but fuck me, that makes me want to sack Scrivener off, sit on the sofa the rest of the day and devour the book. But I won't, even though it pains me, instead we will examine what made Scheuerer's opening so compelling.

"Far below the darkest waters, in a cell made of bones, a creature was born. [*The promise of an important birth and the question of who the baby is.*] She was the only one of her kind [*the promise of a unique and special birth makes it even more tantalizing*] to have entered the realm in such way: on the cold, bloody stones of Saddoriel's prison. In the waning torchlight, her mother, the prisoner, closed her lilac eyes. Bracing herself against the raw beat of lingering pain, she already sensed the death song that hummed within her daughter [*the promise that not only was the birth important, but now the kid is special and has abilities*], as strong [*promise of power*] as the ancestors before her. It was the quiet promise [*a literal promise to the reader of something to come*] of poignant keys and mesmerizing notes: magic. [*the promise of magic to come*] Ready to be honed into one of the most powerful weapons [*the promise of danger and war and competition*] known to the realms above, belonging to a cyren of the vast and ancient deep. The prisoner [*the promise of a conclusion to prison either through death or escape, leaving the reader with a question*] gazed down at the small being in the crook of her elbow. In all her centuries of existence, she had never seen a newborn up close before, and this one was *hers* [*the promise that this relationship is special and important and the plot will circle here again*]. She peered at the tiny, pink face in wonder. Without the glimmer of scales at her temples, or the dark fingernails that turned to talons, the infant could have been human."

So you don't have to be overt with questions, like "what would Karen do?" That's far too much exposition. Instead, Scheuerer weaves questions and promises through by giving snippets of information and detail without revealing everything. We have no names, save Saddoriel. We just have promises of what's coming.

The Last Page

Of course, you could also apply some of the same deconstruction tactics to the last page too. If the book is in a series, then there should be promises and hooks for what's coming in later books. Ask yourself:

- Was the ending satisfying? If so, why?
- What was the setup that paid off?

- The last line, much like the first, is usually poignant or meaningful. Deconstruct it. How was the meaning created?
- Is it plot connected? Is it beautifully written?
- Or is it philosophical?
- Does it mirror the beginning?
- What plotlines did the author conclude?
- What was left open for the reader to interpret?
- If the ending doesn't land, why? What was missing? What should have happened instead?

Careful here, there's a difference between wanting more as a reader because it didn't end how you wanted it to, and feeling genuinely cheated by the author.

For example, I recently watched the last season of my favorite TV show in recent times, Killing Eve. The fourth and final season promised to be epic. However, there was a lesbian love story between the main two characters. I turned to my wife as we hit play on episode one and said, "Are you ready for the lesbians to die in an unhappy ending?"

She gritted her teeth and nodded. And of course, come the finale, Villanelle and Eve (after being teased for four straight seasons) get together fifteen minutes before the episode ends. But surprising literally no one, Villanelle gets shot and killed in the last thirty seconds of the episode. Worse, that is it. She's dead. The show pops up a "the end" sign and the credits roll. "#@?!%$ jokers. It's Tara and Willow from *Buffy the Vampire Slayer* all over again.

"Bury Your Gays" folks, a trope that is inconsiderately used throughout the history of literature and media. To date, there's only a minute number of queer folk who have gotten a happy ending in mainstream media. The problem with Killing Eve is that the promise didn't meet the payoff. Yes, I knew one of them would die, but that's not what the show promised for four back-to-back seasons. If you tease your readers with something (like a sapphic romance), for the love of all things literary, give it to them and let them keep it. Don't do a Killing Eve and rip it away three seconds later. All you'll do is piss off your readers.

Can you imagine if a romance author did that?

Sigh.

Back to fiction.

Your Last Line

Last lines have different uses depending on whether they're in a standalone book—in which case they had better be ending on a complete and conclusive point. Or if it's the last line in the first book of a series, the chances are you're going to have a hook that leads you to the next book. If it's the last book in a series, then like a standalone, it better conclude comprehensively.

Example

Keepers by Sacha Black.

First line

"Father always said not to trust a Fallon that can't keep the Balance. I should have listened."

Last Line

"This creature, this Fallon, can't be flying across the square because I killed him with my own hands. Father was right. But he should have added, '...Even the dead ones.'

The creature slows, beats his dark wings and hovers at my eye line.

"Victor.""

The reason I'm showing you both the first and last lines is because they're a sort of echo of each other. They're a question and, finally, an answer. In the first line, although there's no question mark, there's a question inherent in the line because of the lack of information.

> Father always said not to trust a Fallon that can't keep the Balance. [Affirmative and black and white statement] I should have listened. [Insinuation: something went wrong]

The first line foreshadows the ending that there's a Fallon she can't and shouldn't trust. We want to know what went wrong. The contradiction elicits the question. The last line gives the reader "the who" and the answer to what went wrong. Endings like this always feel satisfying to me. They give that sense of inevitability.

In *Sweet and Bitter Magic* by Adrienne Tooley, she opens with a sentence about how her protagonist can't taste (this is because of a curse). Then, in the last line, there's a description of the exquisite taste she's experiencing. A fantastic and direct mirror of the character's start and end state.

In *Trey*, the last book in my YA fantasy trilogy, there's a completely different kind of last line. Much more philosophical. But then, this is the conclusion to a series. I wanted to remind the reader of the theme, the point, and the journey they'd been on from book one to here. There's no need to open any more loops or create any hooks. Everything has to be shut down. Which is why I went for a more thematic last line. There are three last lines, of sorts. The final book is written from three points of view. The protagonist, the love interest, and a news reporter. Each character has a final chapter, but the very last line is the news reporter. This is because the book opens with the reporter and I love coming full circle on things like openings and closings. It gives me that shivery feeling of complete-ness. It tingles real good.

> "This is Tarkin Tavas signing off from CogNews TV for the
> final time.
> 　May you forever carve your own destinies."

So not only do you actually get Tarkin giving a "knowing" narration as he says "final time" you also get the philosophy. May you carve your own destiny. The big conflict in the trilogy comes from the character's having their destiny determined by the villain. They want free of that, and that's what they fight for. Which is why I liked a last reference to the future and to hope for those characters.

STEP 2 DECONSTRUCT SUMMARY

Where we pissed off Marie Kondo, vomited questions, got forensic with words, hacked shit up, and found holy grails.

- Deconstruction is actually pattern recognition.
- At its heart, deconstruction is literally asking questions.

The process:

- Step 1: Feel the Feels
- Step 2: Mark When You Feel
- Step 3: Analyze
- Step 4: Develop Awareness
- Read Every Single Word
- Use Sticky Tabs

If it helps, this is the system I use:

- Pink: character tools

- Orange: obvious tools such as foreshadowing, subtext, something structure related
- Yellow: narration / voice
- Green: description
- Blue: dialogue
- Purple: relationship
- Other purple: emotion and anything else

Use the who, what, when, why and how method of questioning.

- **Who:** who is saying what you're reading? Protagonist, narrator, side character? Someone else?
- **When:** when is this passage in the book? Does the placement mean something? Is it in an emotional scene? Does it correlate with a pivotal story structure moment? i.e., inciting incident, dark night of the soul, the climax, etc.
- **What:** what is it? Description, dialogue, narrative summary, inner thought, personification, a juxtaposition, subversion, characterization? What device or tool is the author using?
- **Why:** why did they use that specific tool? Was it to make you feel a certain way? To reveal information? To make you empathize with an awful character? To draw glorious rainbow-colored images in your mind? To make something resonate? Why was this moment in particular powerful?
- **How:** this is the tricky bit. This is where you understand what the author has done. How did the author create the effect? Combine the answers to all the other questions and dig to the simplest unit to discover the how.

- For pattern recognition, collect sentences, organize sentences, ask questions about sentences, imagine what else you can do with what you found.
- Good deconstruction drills down to the simplest unit possible.

INTERMISSION

It's go time, darlings.

If you haven't already started devouring the book you chose, pop this one down—but not for too long. We're not done yet. But I want you to read a fiction book alongside this one so you can implement the techniques we've discussed in the last section. It's time to read and deconstruct.

Off you trot, read all the words. Figure out all the patterns.

Then come back because it's implementation time...

STEP 3 IMPLEMENT

3.0 IMPLEMENT

Where we repeat shit over and over, discover that practice really does make perfect, and stick our fingers in the mucky market pie.

If you've read any of my other books, you'll have heard me discuss the eye-twitch-inducing misquote that surrounds Malcolm Gladwell. It goes like this: it takes 10,000 hours of practice to master a skill.

Wrong.

That's not even remotely close to what he meant. Why? It's not just practice you need, it's *purposeful, focused, intentional* practice. It's the intention behind the practice that creates a master in a field.

This is how I phrased it previously:

"If you want to run a marathon, you don't just pull Lycra pants on and go for a jog hoping for the best; no, that will lead to a case of shin splints, runners' trots and probably projectile vomiting three miles in. You create a plan, you know how many times a week you need to run and what distance each of those runs needs to be. You intentionally train and practice.

You focus on a very specific mile goal and you work your way methodically towards the finish line. The same is true for writers." Sacha Black, *The Anatomy of Prose.*

What about Stephen King? He's also got something to say on the topic of reading.

"If you want to be a writer, you must do two things above all others: read a lot and write a lot." Stephen King, *On Writing: A Memoir of the Craft.*

Like Gladwell's misquote, King failed to mention the fact that it's not just about reading any old words. If it were as simple as picking up any book and consuming words, then your average five-book-a-year reader could write like Tolstoy. If you want to improve your writing, then it's about reading with intention, with a purpose, and a goal in mind.

Gladwell has clarified that the 10,000-hour rule...

"Is a metaphor for the extent of commitment necessary in cognitively complex fields." Malcolm Gladwell, YouTube. Link in the resource section.

For anyone not reading this digitally, you can download the resource pack to go with this book, where I include more examples of deconstruction. Grab that here: sachablack.co.uk/bestseller

Whether you've implemented as we've gone, decided to have a bash once you're finished, or if you're hoping that having perused the book you'll make small tweaks as you go, it's time to get down and dirty.

Think about it. When you learn to talk or walk, you can't spend all of your time thinking. Eventually, at some point, you have to move your lips around a word and place one foot after the other.

The other thing to say about implementation is that it takes practice. The first time you walk, you wobble, fall on your butt and we get bruises. Expect the same with your writing. You can't deconstruct once and expect perfection.

Try. Fail. Learn. Fail better. Try harder. Learn deeper. Success.

I know for me, I've found a tool that at face value seemed amazing. Then I tried to use it. I slotted it into my voice and it just went limp like a... Well, anyway, it sounded warped and weird. As if I were coughing out a sentence instead of letting it flow.

This is okay. This is progress. Finding what doesn't work for you and your voice is just as useful as finding what does.

That's why I started the book categorizing three different flavors of best seller. Not everyone wants to read, let alone write, the same type of story. It's why we deconstruct and why we absolutely have to implement.

This is a process and a system. It doesn't work unless you use it.

It's time to turn the data into tools and the tools into words.

Finding Other Sources to Study

Just a brief final note to say the world is your oyster or some cheesy bollocks like that.

Throws arms out

Don't limit yourself, babe. This deconstruction methodology can be used across any medium or format of story. You wanna learn to write more lyrically? Read poems or song lyrics. You want to improve the hooks and pacing of your story? Maybe watch and deconstruct really addictive episodic TV shows. Book to film translation your dream? Then don't fuck about, deconstruct movies in the same genre you write.

The amazing thing about words is that they're everywhere. It's how we communicate, how we pass information, how we sing and teach. All words are valid and there's always something to be gleaned from the text you encounter.

Consider:

- Famous quotes
- Song lyrics
- Poetry
- Short stories and flash fiction
- Film and TV
- Consider sales copy
- Book blurbs
- Newsletter emails
- Short stories and flash fiction

I am always scanning for things to deconstruct and genuinely have folders and text files with snippets and quotes from all the items I've suggested.

World. Oyster.

Let's be 'aving ya.

3.1 IMPLEMENTATION GAMES

Let us begin at the beginning. With first sentences.

As you know, I'm a little obsessed with collecting first sentences. They're often underutilized. It's the first impression your reader gets. And while, yes, they'll (hopefully) soldier on through another 3-400 pages of story, if you don't hook them with that opening gambit, then you can kiss 3-400 pages of reader joy goodbye.

First lines can do so. Many. Things. Which is why I want to start there.

Observations

Here's the thing about this whole deconstruction game. You can gather lots of information and useful tools by deconstructing individual sentences. But you can also gather lots more information when you compare half a dozen or more.

Unlikeable Characters

I don't know about you, but there's something exquisitely

intoxicating about an author making you love a character who you're supposed to hate. So let's look at a collection of first lines from books containing grumpy/unlikable characters. We're going to use the what, when, why and how structure for analysis.

Wallace Prior

> "Patricia was crying. Wallace Prior hated it when people cried." *Under the Whispering Door* by T. J. Klune.

What

What is Klune saying? He's started with an upset character and a second character with no empathy. It's a narrative description of character actions and opinions.

When

When is less relevant here, we know it's at the beginning.

Why

Now, that's an interesting question and one that brings us our first set of tools. Much in the same way, good character descriptions tell us something about the character's being and personality. This opening gambit tells us not just WHAT is going on, but something about Wallace's character too. So, Klune has made the sentence work double already.

Wallace is clearly unsympathetic, and not a nice person if he hates other people crying. I suspect this is why Klune wrote the opening line the way he did. A controversial statement that says more about the protagonist than it does about the character crying. We're (as readers) either going to dislike Wallace from the outset, or, if you're on the darker-sarcasm end of the scale, you're probably sniggering at the line. Having read the book, I can also tell you that this line smacks of the tone of the book too.

Okay, but how?

How

How did Klune create such an impactful sentence?

The first line: "Patricia was crying" is a statement of action. Not too interesting, but let's keep going because I see shiny gold on the horizon. Klune brings an emotion—and a powerful one that usually evokes reader empathy right into the opening line. However, the magic is in the next line. "Wallace Price hated it when people cried." Here, it's less about the rhythm and word choice Klune has made and more about how he's employing characterization.

Klune uses character opinion, specifically the opinion of another character's emotion, to create characterization. How, how, how? Well, in isolation, Patricia crying is pretty meaningless. It's the first line of a book and we don't know who this person is, so no one cares. But the fact the protagonist has an opinion on the crying gives meaning to the first line. Protagonist's opinions tell readers things. Hating crying is also not a socially accepted norm. We're expected to comfort those in pain or upset. So his opinion is unexpected. In raw device terms, and boiling it down to the simplest unit, Klune did the following:

Statement of character action/emotion + unexpected and controversial protagonist opinion on said emotion.

But then what? How do we go from having deconstructed what an author has done to actually being able to use what we've found? We put it into practice, that's how. Let's take a grumpy, unlikeable character from a completely different story, one we're going to make up right now, and create a first line. Say they're a masterful magician who hates magic. We're going to use the tools Klune and then each subsequent author used in turn.

Original:

> "Patricia was crying. Wallace Prior hated it when people cried." *Under the Whispering Door* by T. J. Klune.

Klune's tools: Statement of character action/emotion + unexpected and controversial protagonist opinion on said emotion.

Sacha uses tools:

> The peasant was begging again. Earl hated it when peasants begged for magic.

Archibald James Portendorf

> "Archibald James Portendorf disliked stairs. With their ludicrous lengths, ever leading up, as if in some jest." *A Master of Djinn* by P. Djèlí Clark.

What

> *Squeals* Did you notice a similar pattern?
> *"Archibald James Portendorf hated stairs."* Well, would you lookie-look at that? Clark has started his novel with an opening sentence where the character dislikes something, just like Klune. In terms of a WHAT, we have a pissed off character moaning about stairs.

Why

Well, because when a character dislikes something mundane and inoffensive, it tells us something about that character. It tells us they're probably a little highly strung. If the opening impression of a new person is them moaning about something, you're going to assume they're a grumpy bastard.

The next sentence is a more detailed description of his issues with stairs.

How

How does Clark create such a powerful grumpy character feeling so quickly?

First up, he makes a controversial statement. No one hates stairs. Sure, they might be a trifle inconvenient for the less fit. Even a sweat inducing exercise, but hate? Bit strong, mate. It tells us Archibald is a miserable grump of a character. Then Archibald continues to explain and elaborate on the stairs, labeling them ludicrous and to personify them by accusing them of taking the mick out of him. So we have a tool here: personification of the inanimate object causing the protagonist irritation. So boiling it down to the simplest unit we have:

Controversial opinion + Personification (and demonizing of protagonist's irritation).

The similarities between the two are interesting already. Both have protagonists who have a dislike of something most wouldn't bat an eyelid at. That's a connection. Not quite a pattern yet, though.

Original:

"Archibald James Portendorf disliked stairs. With their ludicrous lengths, ever leading up, as if in some jest." *A Master of Djinn* by P. Djèlí Clark.

Clark's tools: Controversial opinion + Personification and demonizing of protagonist's irritation.

Sacha uses tools: Earl hated magic. It always caused problems, and if you weren't completely precise in your application, it would fuck you in the ass like your bitch of an ex.

The Hating Game

> "I have a theory. Hating someone feels disturbingly similar to being in love with them." *The Hating Game* by Sally Thorne.

What

Now this sentence is a little different. The previous two were about characterization. This character is more likeable than the last two, and certainly likeable earlier in the book. However, she's still a little madame, and is deeply flawed. Enough that we dislike parts of her.

This time, the first sentence is the statement of incoming opinion: "I have a theory." Then she lays her opinion on us. "Hating someone feels disturbingly similar to being in love with them."

Why

Well, first up, this is foreshadowing. She's essentially telling us the plot of the book before it begins. Clever, if you ask me. But she's also laying out the character's beginning mindset, ready for a mirror image or confirmation at the end of the book.

As we've seen from the other two sentences, character opinion tells us something about that character. And it does in this case too. Another thing to note is that in all three cases, there are two sentences making up the complete opening phrase. Like the last two, the protagonist's statement here is a controversial one. Hate and love are two ends of a continuum. Hating someone shouldn't be like loving them. It should be the complete opposite.

How

How does she create the effect? First up, she's using a juxtaposition. Smashing love and hate far closer together than they should be. It's surprising, unexpected—there's that word again. All three authors did something unexpected in their first lines. I also think Thorne's choice of the word "disturbingly" is crucial here. It implies that the protagonist is uncomfortable with her revelation. It smacks of the brewing shitstorm to come. She, the character, is disturbed. Meaning she's uncomfortable and doesn't like it. Excellent, that only means one thing... trouble for the protagonist and that's something readers love. That word is also the crux of her opinion. Thorne could have said "weirdly" or left out the word entirely, but it wouldn't have had as significant of an impact. Let's boil it down to the simplest unit.

Statement + unexpected character opinion = foreshadowing + characterization.

Original:

"I have a theory. Hating someone feels disturbingly similar to being in love with them." *The Hating Game* by Sally Thorne.

Thorne's tools: Statement + unexpected character opinion = foreshadowing + characterization.

Sacha uses tools:

I've decided Magicians are wrong about magic. It's sentient. It behaves too much like my vengeful ex-girlfriend not to be.

Reflecting on all three sentences so far, all the authors have done the following to create their unlikable characters:

- Used the word hate or dislike
- Opened with character opinion
- Did something controversial or unexpected

Three is a pattern. It means something that they're all using these tools. On to the last opening sentence.

Lemony Snicket

"If you are interested in stories with happy endings, you would be better off reading some other book." *The Bad Beginning: A Series of Unfortunate Events* by Lemony Snicket.

What

Here, at face value, we have something completely different. A statement talking directly to the reader and trying to dissuade them from reading the book. It's written in second person. Snicket is addressing the reader directly, breaking the fourth wall. While the content of the sentence is different to the others, in that it's issuing a warning, it holds the same irreverent tone. It dismisses the reader.

Why

Second person is a tricky tool to master. It reminds the reader they're reading. This pulls them out of the story—a risk. But, when used successfully, it can draw the reader deeper into the story than any other tool. It can make the reader part of the story. Second person, with deep fourth wall breaks, can create an air and tone of superiority, a godlike character, or a character with supreme arrogance. And that creates an unlikeable character, at least at first.

How

Fourth wall breaks, second person... But like the other first lines, it also uses the unexpected. Characters aren't supposed to address the reader, they're fictional. And when they do address the reader, they certainly aren't supposed to tell them not to read the book.

Second person + fourth wall break + unexpected reader command

Original:

"If you are interested in stories with happy endings, you would be better off reading some other book." *The Bad Beginning: A Series of Unfortunate Events* by Lemony Snicket.

Snicket: Second person + fourth wall break + unexpected reader command
Sacha uses tools:

If you think this is a story about how great and wonderful magic is because it gives everyone happily ever after's, you might want to reread the title.

All four of the sentences I created use the same tools in roughly the same order as the original sentences. But they're completely different, unconnected, about different characters, content and unrecognizable when placed next to the original. Taken in isolation, these first lines can show us individual tools and techniques for creating powerful first lines. But taken

together, they show us patterns and a deeper level of understanding. Granted, some of these implementations work better
than others. I'm not keen on the flow of some. But hopefully
you can see how to break something into the smallest units and
pluck the tool for your own use.

Read.

Deconstruct.

Implement.

3.2 THE GOD-AWFUL CONVERSATION NO ONE WANTS TO HAVE

Let's talk about the dreaded Venn Diagram of what you want, versus what the market wants, where that merges and how to have your cake and eat it. Because here's the thing, a lot of us will smile and nod at this conversation and question. We'll give a shit-eating grin because we're exceptionally good at looking like we agree and understand the concept. But most of us either don't, or we do, but don't want to accept it.

Myself included.

I fell into the latter bracket for a looooong time. It's taken an exquisitely painful amount of time to get here.

But first...

The Awful Question No One Wants to Answer Honestly

I know some people hate talking about goals, but bear with me a second.

What is your goal for the book you're writing?

Seems like an innocuous question, right?

It's not.

This is about to get ugly.

Takes a deep breath

What do you want? Really, truly? Because so many of us are afraid to admit what we want. But try... for me? Pretty please?

Even if you can't say it out loud. Stop, take a breath and whisper to the universe. It can be a secret, pressed between the woody—or digital—mulch of these pages.

Generally speaking, what writers want can fall into a couple of categories:

Write the best book they can, or sell a fuckload of books.

Now, before anyone throws a squirrel at me, yes, there are a ton of nuances beyond that. Especially for those writers wanting to complete a memoir or maybe a writer who just wants to prove they can actually finish a project, blah, blah. The list is endless.

But for writers wanting a career, there tends to be this pull between the goal of writing the best book possible or making money.

Am I saying these two things are separate? No. Don't be so black and white. Of course, you can have a brilliantly written book that's also a best seller.

But. There is a difference in approach.

Sell a Fuckload of Books Goal

There is something you have to understand in your bones. We writers are not our audience. We're not our readers.

I'm asking what your goal is because if you want to sell a boatload of books, and make loads of money, then your approach to writing—and therefore the deconstruction you're about to do should have a different focus than if your goal is to write the best book possible.

Readers of each genre want something specific. That does not always connect with what we want to write as authors.

I'll say that again.

Readers of each genre want something specific. That does not always connect with what we want to write as authors.

I hear a lot of authors say they read the best sellers in a genre and don't like the books and can't understand why they're selling so well.

Oh, honey. I'll tell you why, you won't like it... But I'll tell you, anyway.

It's because those authors aren't writing for authors.

They're writing for readers.

They understand what readers of that genre want and need. They know what tickles their good parts and give them tingles. And then in the plot twist of the year, that's exactly what they write.

Shocking, I know.

Now, those authors are also marketing those books fucking well, but this isn't a marketing book, so I won't talk about that end of the process.

I have railed against this for so long.

I don't want it to be true. I hate it.

But. *It is* true.

You could be one of the lucky ones where you don't mind writing exactly what the reader wants—I'm jealous if you are. But if you're not and you find it tricky to write anything other than what your soul desires, then that's okay, too.

I think a lot of this tension comes from the fact that writing starts as a creative outlet for so many of us. So if you *have* to bend and shape a story to fit a particular genre mold, it feels like a job. I left my corporate day job because I hated having a "job"—something about an authority problem, apparently?

Whatever.

The point is, I don't want to write purely about what

someone else wants. I want to write for me. But I also like money.

Fuck, don't tell anyone, but I actually love money. I want to sleep with money, bathe in it, wipe my... I want to shower in it. Spend it. Keep it. Save it.

I want fuckloads of it.

But that means delivering exactly what the reader wants.

So you and I, we have a choice.

We can either deliver precisely what the reader wants and therefore set ourselves up for potential success, or we can write exactly what we want and if that doesn't align to the reader, then... well, you fill in the blank. Remember, "potential" is the key word. You can do all the right things, create a killer campaign and have it still flop. Then again, sometimes you can have a breakout success totally by accident.

Not liking either of these options?

You could always bend the rules and try to find a compromise. Perhaps everyone wins with a compromise, but equally, in every compromise I've ever made, no one was quite as happy as they wanted.

For me, my acceptance of this comes in finding a genre and niche where I can both deliver what the reader wants and still write the stories I desire. But that has been a process of experimentation and research... a lot of research. And it took time. I know it's not what you want to hear, but it's the truth.

For the goal of most sales, the best option is to write to "market". But you know what? I hate that phrase. It causes so many eyeball twitches and internal rebellions that I think we should do away with it. Instead, reframe that puppy.

The best option for selling boatloads of books is to "Write to Reader." There. I've said it. If it hasn't been already, someone coin that shit immediately.

The moment you become a writer, your brain changes the way it reads. Even if you're not reading with the intention to deconstruct, you're intuitively reading differently because you're not just a reader anymore. You're a writer and writers have a different lens than readers.

Once you've been writing for a few years, it's an enlightening experience to go back and read a book you used to love. Your opinion may have changed, or at least you'll likely see it in a different light.

I don't want to have a conservation about luck and market timing, that is not the purpose of this book. To acknowledge it, yes, sometimes there are market pressures, unforeseen technological advances, zeitgeists that hit and thus a book becomes a lightning bolt one in a million. I'm not denying that. But those are one in a million odds and I'd rather work on upping the odds in my favor by doing shit I can control. Does that mean I don't want lightning bolt success? Are you out of your fucking mind? Of course I want it. But you and I are the humblest of writing worker bees. We can't control technological changes, we can't force a zeitgeist, we're not Thor, and this isn't a Marvel movie where we can shoot lightning bolts from our testicles.

There are some facts we need to accept.

To sell a fuckload of books, you have to deliver what the reader wants. It doesn't matter *how* you do that, only that you do.

Some writers can feel their way through a genre and deliver exactly what the reader wants. They just know. Others (like me) have to be more intentional. I have to study first and then weave my findings through like I'm the fairy-fucking-godmother of the genre.

Does giving the reader exactly what they want guarantee success? I wish. If it were that simple, I'd be a gazillionaire by now and we'd all be rolling in Netflix deals. Logically though, making sure you're hitting all the most wanted genre needs sets you up for *potential* success. Then you need a tip-top, targeted marketing campaign, a brilliant cover, even better copy, a knack for advertising and finding readers.

Simple, right?

And if you don't know me well enough by now, then let me assure you that "simple" was profoundly sarcastic.

I Want to Write the Best Book Possible

Mmkay, so your goal is to write the best book possible?

Good.

Excellent, even.

But first, a harder question. What does "best" look like? The only way to be the best or to write the best book is to know what "best" looks like.

To be the best, you have to measure "best".

Even if that's an intuitive feeling and gut, I just know. What does best look like to you? Is it acceptance from traditional publishing gatekeepers? Is it NYT best seller status? Is it a million books sold? (See the above section and blend the two). Is it a high level of reviews? A huge fandom visibly posting on social media. Is it one fan outside your friends and family? Is it winning an award? Is it reviews that always mention beautiful prose? Is it having the best banter and dialogue between characters? Is it having a twist no one saw coming? Is it writing a book to the best of your personal writing skill ability? Is it being number one in your genre? What is best?

Name it, define it, be at one with it.

If you're wanting to write the best book and wanting to measure that by numbers of sales, then you have a disconnect.

It's not that "best seller" means it's inferior quality, far from it. But that's not the metric to measure your goal. Sales is a measure of market desire, a measure of one's ability to market effectively, to write good copy, have an excellent cover, the size of your existing audience, and, of course, your ability to include all the aspects the genre readers want and desire. And last, lest we forget, that ineffable sprinkling of unicorn sugar-tit sparkle.

So if you want to write the best book possible, and you're measuring that by sales, you're setting yourself up to fail because your goal is not, in fact, to write the best book, it's selling as many copies as possible.

Semantics?

Maybe.

But I've had to learn this the hard way. If I'm not crystal clear in my expectations, in the goals I lay down and the metrics I used to measure them, shit can get messy real fast.

A final, but important point here. There's no right answer. If you want to sell lots of books, don't be ashamed of that. So many creatives avoid talking about money and figures and their actual goals because of some made up bullshit about what "creatives should be and what they should want". Well, fuck that. I want to sell a fuck-bucket load of books and I'm not afraid to say it. I also want to write good books. So I need to make sure my desires as an author and writer align closely enough to my genre choices to create the potential for success.

Let's figure out how to do that, shall we?

3.3 DECONSTRUCTING THE MARKET

I almost, *almost* didn't include this section. It felt... businessy instead of crafty. But if we're deconstructing books and genres to learn how to do what the best sellers do, then in the spirit of completeness, we should also look at the market the books are in. Let me just state for the record, this is not a marketing chapter. I'm not teaching you marketing, only how to look at and deconstruct the market.

Why bother?

Because the market is where you sell the book and where the reader will find it. And while you can get a lot of information and patterns from the books you deconstruct, a book is not just the words you read. It's a package, a cover, a marketing plan, a blurb. It's a feeling and a theme, it's a genre and an emotion bestowed upon readers.

Many people talk about the market—understanding it, researching it, moving with the ebbs and flows of it as it changes. But I also think it's one of the hardest things to get your head around when you're a new writer. To truly understand where you're dropping your book and what that means, not just for your marketing and business efforts, but your craft, too. That's the bit most writers miss. They think marketing comes after they've written the book.

If I haven't ruffled your feathers yet, get ready. Just know I'm doing this not to break up with you, but to encourage you to be a better writer.

Note: I reference YA as a genre in this section, I'm fully aware that "YA" really refers to the age of the protagonist rather than an actual genre like "fantasy" however, I'm using it as a catchall to reference books that fall under the category of YA because it's easier, and I can, so...

Blows raspberry

Second, I'm going to give several examples from YA in this section specifically because that's the genre I write in. I don't want to talk about deconstructing other markets because I haven't deconstructed them. I don't know those markets as well as I know mine. But I'm showing you the methods used so you can apply them to your genre.

Market Mistakes

A lot of writers think that deconstructing the market is a one and done afternoon jobby.

"Oh, well, big wig indie told me to 'know my genre' so I'm spending the afternoon looking at the charts and waiting for the postie to dump the ten crates of books I just ordered on my doorstep."

Oh, dear sweet child.

Okay, yes. You can, in fact, get a lot of data from spending the afternoon looking at the charts. But you can't *know* the market. At least, not in the way you need to. Not if your aim is to set yourself up for potential success. Not if you want to create that delicious kerching sound and flood your bank account with dollar bills.

No.

This takes time.

You have to watch and leer at the market, salivate over the latest releases while pondering what's keeping those three smug little fuckers in the top charts for weeks.

Sounds a little seedy, but stick with me. There is, I suppose, an aspect of being a voyeur with knowing your market.

A lot of advice is blanket: know your market, learn your market, understand your market.

But what in titty-heaven's name does that actually mean?

I want to give you a framework to help you look at your market. And in my humblest of experience, breaking things down usually helps. So. Let's look at the market for what it is: a changeable beast.

There are elements of the market that are in a constant flux, other elements that shift less quickly and others that don't shift at all.

I've tried to cut the "market" into pieces multiple times and the most effective way I've found is to think of it in layers of change.

Layer One: Shit that changes frequently = the books at the top of the charts.

This is both a perk and a problem. An author could be doing a random promotion and have shot their book to the top of the charts—now, the perk is that this is useful information. If you know they're actively promoting their work, they might make a suitable target for your own advertising—but if the book then plummets to the bottom of the charts a couple of days later, then it tells you two things:

1. The author didn't have a solid marketing plan, only a one-off promotion that wasn't backed up.
2. If you only look at the charts once, you might go away thinking that their book was one of the top

books or authors to watch, rather than an author who did a time-limited promo.

Okay, but does that mean you have to track the charts in spreadsheets and lists?

No. Not unless you get kicks out of that stuff. A lot of the way I work is by consuming data, then thinking about it. I whip out my best voyeur, watch the charts for weeks, and internalize who and what is at the top and for how long. If you can't do that and you need to write stuff down, do it. You'll have more accurate data that's less susceptible to mom-brain like me.

Make your process work for you.

Alternatively, there are several systems and data reports you can get and use to give you this info. Although remember they're only as good as the software they're built on, and nothing really compares to using your own eyes to watch the charts. My personal favorites are Alex Newton's K-Lytics reports and Nat Connors Kindletrends.

With layer one, it's easy to get the data as it's continually live, but that also means it's continually updating. You need both the "what's hot now" data and the more enduring, "how long has that been hot for" information because this tells you about the sustainability and volatility of the market and therefore whether you can use the information in your marketing.

Layer Two: Shit that changes less frequently = trends, covers, new niches

There are elements of the market that are slower to change, but change nonetheless. These are more likely to be enduring trends like popular cover styles or hot categories and upcoming niches. For example, right now (as I write this in 2022) we're seeing an enduring rise/explosion of enemies to lovers trope usage in YA and other genres too. This will stick around for a while. It's been around for a few months, and it doesn't appear to be going anywhere either. Another example was the move towards more crime and mystery in YA. Undoubtably, both will change. Perhaps fake dating will become *the* trope. Maybe we'll return to dystopian being "the thing". Or, perhaps it will be something else. But this is an example of a middle ground aspect of markets that hang around a while and then, in a proper Thanos-style finger click, the market shifts and a new trend appears.

There are other aspects that shift like this too:

Covers

For example, when *Divergent* and *The Hunger Games* (and all things dystopian) were the height of popularity in YA, it was all about having a big symbol on the front cover. Now for indies, a lot of the covers are photo manipulation with a girl (or protagonist) front and center with color-branded magic wisps and an appropriate scene setting behind them. I'm speaking in generalizations, of course. Steampunk is a subset of fantasy, but the covers would be different. This is why knowing, not just your market and genre, but also the sub niches you fall into, is so important.

Each genre has its own unique trends. I spoke to Meg Jolly, USA Today Best-selling Author. She said:

"Broadly speaking, in the crime genre, there was a running joke about the fact every book used to have a woman walking away in a red coat in front of a moody background. But it was done to death in some crime sub genres. Now, although most crime covers still have some sort of shadowy figure walking away, they're also landscape/setting focused because the landscape and locale can be as much a character as the actual characters, especially in regionally focused crime.

For fantasy, interestingly, it's going the other way. For the past few years, covers have been very character focused. Most used photo manipulation, or heavily illustrated photo manipulation. Some were purely illustrated characters. Over the past year it's shifted a lot towards symbols on covers again and typography covers especially."

We continued the discussion, noting that what might work for e-books doesn't necessarily work for paper or hardback. More to the point, indie books don't always follow the same trend as traditionally published books. So it's important to examine or try to figure out whether the books you're looking at are trad or indie. More on that below.

Meg said:

"In fantasy, character covers still perform well for e-book but a lot of authors in the more romantic fantasy genres specifically, are finding a lot of success with typography hardcover and paperbacks. Traditionally published books err towards the latter too, so I wonder if that's a perceived value thing. Because 'trad = high perceived value products'. When we [indies] emulate that, readers get the same feel."

Note the type and style of covers you see in your genre too. Do they have people on the cover? Is it photo manipulation? Graphics? Is there a core set of colors that you see most often— hint, there usually is. What are the fonts like? Big and bold? Swirly and dainty? Where does the author's name go? At the top? The bottom? Are the fonts and typography in a similar set of colors? Do they have quotes on the front? Are they plain? Deconstruct every ounce of detail you can out of the cover. Make a note of the patterns and hand this puppy to your cover designer.

Content

I've briefly mentioned tropes, but the tone, atmosphere and what's acceptable to a genre can change too. For example, the tone, quantity and explicitness of "sex" in YA has changed drastically over the last decade. Previously, no mentions of actual bedroom romps were acceptable. It was always a case of fade to black. Now, there's on-page sex in a lot of YA books. We have TV shows like *Sex Education* and *Skins*, which have been more explicit than anything before. Following the market, keeping up with reading the books in your genre is essential, otherwise you can miss these moving trends and reader expectations.

Other Items

There are other more nuanced aspects of the market that shift too. For example, book lengths. Genres wax and wane. Young Adult used to have a strict criterion for expected page length and word count. But over the years, we've had big hits like *Priory of the Orange Tree* by Samantha Shannon clocking in at over eight hundred pages. A lot of Sarah J. Maas' work is long and over five hundred pages too. Though Maas might be a controversial example, her work has often been argued as adult or new adult. Definitive age classification aside, a *lot* of teens read her work, and it did affect the genre.

Anyhoo, those are just two examples. It's important to watch things like page count as readers have expectations. They want what they want. Big hits from big named authors can shift and change the trend. Teens don't always want a quick read, sometimes they want to sink into a world.

And what of other shifts? I'll be honest, I spend half my waking hours with blinkers on ignoring the world and focusing on the things that bring me joy. But apparently, not being an antisocial pen monkey helps you understand the societal impact on a genre too.

As the social and political stances wax and wane in the wider world, it trickles into fiction. For example, in YA specifically, there was a proliferation of stories with young romantic relationships considered dubious and not positive in their nature. This led to a change in expectation. Now, many young readers expect explicit consent to be in the book (even if it's only a single line) and also a heavy lean toward less toxic relationships and more positive authenticity and role model relationships.

Layer Three: Shit that never changes = the core and heart of a genre

Consistently Consistent

Then there are the elements of a market that never change. I see these aspects as the elements that really make up the core or heart of that genre. For example, YA means the protagonist is 12-18. If you had a protagonist aged 25, it's not YA, it's adult. That doesn't change. It's part of the definition of YA. If you take out the "serious" crime from a crime book, you don't have a crime book anymore. If you set a historical romance in modern day Britain, you don't have a historical novel. If you don't have a happily ever after, it's not romance.

There's something else that doesn't change, too. What a reader wants. Now, of course, that shifts depending on genre and even sub niches breaking out. But the heart of what a reader wants doesn't change.

A reader wants entertainment and connection. Connection with the characters and entertainment from the story. Of course, entertainment looks different depending on what genre you're in. But entertainment is entertainment.

Okay, I'm going to make some sweeping statements because I'm not diving deep into the mechanics of each genre, but take thrillers. The resounding entertainment a reader wants is the heart-pounding pace of action. Romance is all about swooning and a couple in love. YA is about being seen and understood for the person they're becoming.

But you can go deeper than this. Niche dependent, trope dependent, each one will give the reader something a little different and entertain the reader in a different way. Which is why you have to know your genre intimately.

Distinguishing Trad from Indie

Why would you want to do that? After all, readers don't give two shits whether a book is trad or indie, they only care whether the characters are engaging, the hook is hooky, and the ending is killer.

I know darlings.

I also know that indies spend a good chunk of time trying to write, produce and publish books that are indistinguishable from traditionally published books. So why would we want to undo all of that by trying to wheedle out the indie from the trad? Well, first up, indies are champion marketers. If you find a successful indie in your genre, you need to know because you need to get your observer hat on. Follow that bitch, subscribe to their newsletter, be at one with their marketing methods. Indies also have a lot of flexibility to do promotion and marketing efforts collaboratively, so there's a potential opportunity to grow your network.

But also, if you choose to go into a genre that is dominated by the trad industry, then that will affect and change how you market as an indie author. Instead of looking at indie books and covers, you need to have a cover that mimics the popular trad book covers. Instead of focusing on e-book marketing, perhaps start with paperback. And yes, this is considerably harder for an indie to crack, but it's not impossible.

If you're moving into a heavily indie based genre, the next thing you need to work out is what the dominant publishing model is.

For example, are authors rapidly releasing books into Kindle Unlimited (KU)? Or are they slower to release but still in KU? Maybe the majority of the books are wide. Or perhaps it's a fifty-fifty split and you have more flexibility in your choice of marketing methods. Let's say the dominant model is KU and rapid release, but you don't write fast enough to be what's considered a rapid releaser in that genre. Does that mean you can't succeed?

Nope. Just means you need to dig deeper and see if there are any authors not rapid releasing and find out what marketing methods they're using. Or, you need a bigger backlist, or you need to experiment and find a fresh set of methods that work. Nothing is impossible, but you also have to recognize that every choice you make will change, impact, weaken or increase your potential for success. You need to understand how your market works. You need to deconstruct the release strategies, the marketing methods of the successful authors and their advertising strategies to see whether it's going to fit with you and your skill set and whether you're willing to bend to it or compromise.

Is It a Bird? Is it a Trad? No, it's Indie

The most reliable method of working out whether a book is indie published is to look at the publisher information either on the sales page, or inside the flap of the book. There's a "look inside function" on most stores where you can sneak a peek at the copyright page. If you haven't heard of the publisher—as many indies have a publishing imprint name—then google it. If the publisher or imprint name is only publishing books from one author, you can be pretty confident it's an indie author, if they have lots of authors then chances are it's a small publisher (which could be an indie too) or a medium to large publishing house. It's handy to keep half an eye on publisher names as often imprints focus on a particular type of fiction, so you'll recognize the traditional (trad) competition in your genre.

Deconstructing the Market

Alright, hopefully, I've convinced you it's a good idea to deconstruct your genre and market. Now what? Let's look at some tactics.

The Cesspit

Before you shout, I'm not saying you should check your own reviews—although if you can at least monitor the rating number and maybe get a pal to tell you any patterns appearing in the comments. It'll help you avoid or do more of what readers want/don't want.

It's much safer to check the reviews of popular books in your genre. Why? Cause they're obviously doing something right by being popular. But the reviews will also tell you the elements of the genre they maybe didn't nail.

Don't bother with the one-star reviews. All they tell you is the wrong type of reader picked up the book and kindly left a dog turd in the reviews for other readers to find. You'll get more information from the two- and three-star reviews. Oh, and the five-star reviews too. Five-star reviews tell you what the author did well, and by default, what the market likes and what you should consider including in your own work.

The two- and three-star reviews tell you what the author missed, did wrong or should have considered. Maybe they didn't land a trope effectively, maybe they missed out on an important plot point, maybe the characters always do XYZ in that genre, but this author's characters didn't.

Now, I caution here. Don't take just one three-star review at face value. This is about pattern recognition and noticing when multiple reviews say the same thing, or variations of the same thing. Such as ten people felt the pacing was off, fifty reviews mentioned the characters didn't banter sufficiently for Urban Fantasy, etc.

Look for where multiple readers cite the same or similar aspects of a book. Is a specific trope mentioned? That's important. Do readers comment on how the book made them feel positively? Note that. It's important, there are certain genre expectations readers have about the "feels" they want to come away with. It's also a good place to look for confirmation of your thoughts on a genre. For example, if you know a thriller should be fast-paced, and the reviews all mention how the readers couldn't put the book down, you know the author nailed the pacing. If you want to improve your pacing, it's probably a good book to break down. If you suspect the mystery genre is moving towards including more romantic subplots and that's mentioned in the reviews positively, then you can confirm your gut thoughts. Before anyone gets ruffly feathers, I'm not actually suggesting mysteries are doing that. It was just an example.

Another thing it's useful for, is if you've got an idea of something you want to try, let's say using footnotes sporadically for either humor purposes or to enhance the narrative voice. Perhaps you stumble across a book that uses footnotes, but you read the reviews and find that several reviewers hated that aspect of the book. This tells you something. If it's annoyed the readers enough, they noted it in the review and there are dozens of them saying it, then you have a problem. You can take the risk of upsetting the market and not setting yourself up for potential success as well as you could, but keep the footnotes because you like it and like the effect it creates; or you can remove the footnotes and be assured that you're more aligned to what most readers want.

Reviews might be a cesspit for authors when it's their own book, but it's pure gold when it's another author's books. Without doubt, it's one of the quickest ways to understand what the readers want. Ultimately, anyone can write a book for themselves. But if your goal is to sell a lot of books, then readers are your boss. That's who you have to please.

The Charts and Author Marketing

We've spoken a little about the charts already and that they change constantly, and therefore you need to monitor them. But it bears repeating. If you don't want to hoard spreadsheet data, that's fine. But watch the rankings at least twice a week. Note other things like:

How high the books are charting and their rankings. A note on rankings, though. They're not always accurate or completely indicative of success for a wild number of reasons. But rankings can give you some data. Check both e-book and paperback rankings because they're not the same. If you're in an indie dominated genre (focus on e-book rankings) or a trad dominated genre (focus more on paperback).

If you're heading towards the trad market then while you can check the paperback rankings on some stores, you're probably better off walking down to your local bookstore to see what is charting and what's face out (because usually a publisher pays for this privilege alongside being at the front of a store or on the tables) and what stays in the store consistently.

Another thing to check in the charts is pricing. Some genres price lower or higher than others. This is useful information and you should price accordingly.

I mentioned earlier that following an author who is doing

something you like or charting high in your genre was a good idea. But what does that mean? Let's break that down so you can deconstruct what they're doing.

Stalk That Bitch's Socials

You'll want to be aware of which social they're most active on. What kind of active are they? Do they post regularly? Are they sporadic? What kind of content do they post? More importantly, are they getting lots of interaction? Are there lots of commenters? Do they post video more than static images? Are they doing reels or TikTok's? Do they only talk about their books? Do they share recommendations? Do they share content related to aspects of their books? I.e., a historical fiction author sharing snippets about the time period they write in? Do they do lives? Are they barely on social at all? All of this tells you important and useful information. It does not dictate a marketing method for you or demand that you do exactly what they do. This is just information. If the author you're following is doing lots of video and you hate video and are awkward on camera, I don't suggest doing video because that will come across. You're gathering data, options about what's possible. The more authors you follow and deconstruct in your genre, the more you'll be able to spot patterns about what they all do and therefore, what might work for you, or ideas on how to iterate it to make it work.

Roast Your Inbox

I know. I know. None of us want to fill our inboxes with any more emails. BUT. Signing up to the email newsletter of a popular author in your genre will give you useful marketing data. These are emails worth noting because you'll see the information they're putting out.

- Are their subject lines catchy?
- Do *you* want to open their email?
- What kind of tone do they use?
- Is it consistent with the tone in their books?
- What kind of content do they put out?
- Is it solely about their books?
- Do they post about other things?
- How often do they send emails?
- Do they send emails consistently?
- Do they send more when they launch?
- How much personal information do they share?

Similarly, go to their website.

- Is it static?
- Do they have lots of information on it?
- Do they post blogs?
- Do they have books in a range of genres or just one?
- Do they sell direct?
- What's their shop like?
- Where is their sign up form?
- What's the call to action like on their pop up?
- Do they link out to socials?
- Is it "on brand" in terms of style and content?
- Do they have images of themselves or their books?
- Do they have a contact form and what is it like?

What Advertising do They do?

This is slightly harder to determine. However, for Facebook ads specifically, you can check their Facebook page and the "page transparency" section to see if they're running any. At the time of writing, you'll find this by heading to their author page, clicking "about" and then page transparency is under the about section on the left. But with any tech, this will probably change before I finish typing the sodding sentence.

If you're already following their Facebook page, you may find yourself targeted by one of their ads. Screenshot that motherfucker. Deconstruct the copy. Check the comments section of the ad to see what's said and look for patterns with the images used. Consider whether you would stop and click on their ad. On Amazon, type their name or book title into the search bar. If they're targeting themselves on Amazon, you'll be able to see their books come up with a "sponsored" label. This tells you they're using Amazon's AMS ads system. It's also worth mining their also boughts and checking their author page, particularly on Amazon as they will have a "Customers Also Bought Items By" section which has a list of authors. These are their comp authors and will give you a list of potential authors and books to buy... I mean target... *Ahem, let me correct myself*

It will give you a list of potential authors and books to target.

Another great place to go is Bookbub. Follow comp authors there. You'll get release updates and that will tell you the frequency of their releases, as well as if they are actively reviewing other books and engaging on the platform rather than having a static profile. In fact, just sign up to Bookbub period. You can follow your genre and see who is advertising both the expensive featured deals and the cost per click ads at the bottom of the emails.

The Intangible, Dataless Market Knowledge

Woah, look Sacha. We came along for the ride when you talked about the market because of *hard* data. But now you're trying to tell us there's dataless knowledge?

Side eye

"Umm, yes?"

This is the most difficult aspect of knowing the market to explain. A lot of it is intrinsically based and subconscious. But, try I shall to explain.

First up, where do you hang out? I don't mean your Friday night kink venues. I mean digitally. Knowing where your readers are is essential to helping you read the market. What are your readers saying about the top selling books?

Regardless of which site or location your readers populate, the most popular books are always going to be discussed more than everyone else. But occasionally, there are lesser-known books trending or rising to fame, or being rave reviewed.

So, like:

- What are readers saying?
- What conversations happen around the books?
- Are there common things readers like or always mention that they don't like?
- Check the comments on popular posts. What do the whispers say?
- What do the kids talk about?
- Are there books causing controversy or being mentioned because they do something unusual?
- What is the chatter around the hot book?

The other aspect of this is understanding who your readers are. I know, I know. You hear this all the time.

I get that. But I don't mean the age range or whether they have a degree. That is useful stuff for the hard data and targeting adverts. What I want to know is, how does society affect your target market? For example, I'm a queer woman. The queer market has grown exponentially over the last decade. When I was a teen, there weren't any books with queer teen stories. Or, forgive me, there were, but less than a single handful.

Roll on a decade, same sex marriage is legal in many countries, same sex rights for pensions and adoption and many other aspects are, while not "equal" in the truest sense, significantly better than they were. The impact of that is a proliferation of queer characters and culture seamlessly burrowing into mainstream media and TV. More to the point, the younger generations—millennials in particular—are coming to power. They want change, they want acceptance of diversity, this means more diversity filtering through to mainstream media too.

All of these societal changes affect the market. At first, many young queer books were "coming out stories" as the market matures. That's no longer acceptable. Teens want books with queer and diverse characters where "being gay" isn't the main thrust of the story. It's an element of their being. They want all kinds of stories like any other teen, except they want to be represented too.

If you write in a genre where there's lots of diversity represented, then knowing what political or societal changes are at play can affect the desires and wants of the market. These are typically slow changes. I'm not expecting you to spontaneously make a butt divot on your sofa by consuming ten hours of news content a day. Hell, I don't even watch the news. But being aware of the community of readers you're writing for is important.

This is about watching readers, watching their conversations, knowing what the prominent discussions are. Let's say you notice that there are five books in the top ten legal thrillers, and all of them have immigration stories as their main thread. Okay, that tells you something, that's a hot topic for readers right now, what drove that? Was there a societal impact a year before? A change in immigration law a few months ago that rocked the world? Could you have predicted that more books on this topic would have been published?

Take the "C" word.

Whispers pandemic

Look at how it affected the markets. Dystopian genre sales plummeted at first. Everyone feared the unknown disease and what impact it would have. As the vaccine arrived and society was no longer scared but ready to fight, dystopian sales skyrocketed.

Society affects the market.

What you need to know is how. Follow the changes, follow the impact, watch to see how your genre shifts.

3.4 DECONSTRUCTING WHAT THE READER WANTS

And here we have the sixty-four-million-dollar question. What is it our dear readers want? And how in the name of literary hell do we even figure it out? Does anyone know?

Anyone?

You mean to tell me that no one knows the exact formula for pleasing all their readers? Shocking. Utterly horrifying.

Also, not entirely unsurprising. Because if we had cracked the code to what readers want, we'd all be fucking millionaires, right?

Except we're not. And "what do readers want" is the question I hear most often from authors trying to nail their marketing. So how the hell do you figure it out?

Well, there's research, for one. You know, this entire book of suggestions and ideas? You could, ahh, I dunno, deconstruct some books in your genre and find the commonalities that readers all around the world who love your genre lust over in their wet dreams, and then go do that. You could examine what's selling, and then iterate and replicate. Or you could consider tropes. Are tropes the only way to please readers? Obviously not. But I am going to talk about them now.

I swear I just heard the delightful squeak and pop of half a dozen aneurysms exploding. Why so many people hate tropes, I'll never know. But yo, if you want to create a story that has readers dribbling, then you might wanna change up your attitude.

Tropes are good.

Repeat after me.

TROPES

ARE

GOOD.

Common complaints: tropes are repetitive. Tropes are cliched, tropes are boring.

Bitches be wrong.

I'm going to explain why.

Tropes have a similar feel and core to genre. How?

Genre creates that sense of familiarity that draws readers back to the same shelf in the bookstore time and time again. Genre creates a sense of home, of knowing, of comfort that the reader lusts after. A crime reader reads crime because they want the detective, the mystery, the clues, and the opportunity to be clever, or at least, feel like they're cleverer than the author. But you know one of the ways authors manage that?

Through tropes.

See, there's a lot of confusion about what tropes are and are not.

Throws arms out dramatically

Wipes the whiteboard clear

Clears throat

Tropes have an innate story structure inside them with a buttload of inbuilt tension and conflict. And readers, the little mites, are suckers for a bit of conflict. It's catnip kitty crack for bookworms. Tropes have stakes and known outcomes. Sometimes they even have "must have" scenes required to make the trope land in the juiciest way possible.

Case in point, Enemies to Lovers, is in fact, what I think of as a "proper" trope.

The innate structure in the briefest possible terms: There are two characters who hate each other for [reasons]. Said characters have to come to together or are forced into close quarters for [reasons]. Over time, for [reasons] said characters end up realizing the other isn't so bad after all. The characters fall in love with each other and one usually sacrifices something for the other.

See? Clear story structure and plot. There's an obvious ending and if you're a reader of Enemies to Lovers, then you'll know, no matter what happens and no matter how much the characters might look like they hate each other, it won't be like that in the end. I'm skimming the surface here. But from a reader perspective, why does it work?

What is the psychology behind tropes and why they work so well?

First up, the reader knows what's coming. That's where the similarity between genre and tropes appears. I won't lie, Enemies to Lovers is my absolute all-time favorite trope. Why? Because the characters fucking hate each other to start with. That breeds all kinds of delicious tension and animosity. As a reader, I'm on the edge of my seat salivating over how the hell the author—the crafty bastard—is going to pull this one out of the bag when it seems impossible. This not knowing how, is a question that my reader brain wants to work out. I practically fizz trying to predict what will happen.

What about when the author is a twisted sadist and makes the love interest do something bloody awful to the protagonist? How will I... I mean she (the character obviously) forgive him? There are so many questions, and for anyone with even a basic understanding of psychology, you'll know that the brain is auto-wired to need questions it's posed, answered.

It needs to know in the same way a kid needs the crack

addiction of sugar. BUT MOMMMAAAAYYYY *foot stomp, foot stomp.*

BUT AUTHOR, page turn, page turn.

Charles Darwin argued for survival of the fittest. Only the biggest, strongest, bad ass-est animals survived. Which meant those genes were passed on to new generations. It's the reason we continued to evolve from monkeys into man. It also led to certain desires embedding in our DNA, i.e., the things that would keep us alive and fitter than the rest. If an animal ate lots of fat or high-sugar foods, it meant they had a nice thick fat layer and were more likely to survive the winter. Wealth = survival, beauty = an easier time mating. Privilege = prosperity and evolutionarily speaking, the ability to thrive. These things feed into tropes and it's why they work so well.

Jennifer Lynn Barnes did a fantastic talk on writing for the Id for Romance Writers of America. The talk cost less than ten dollars at the time of writing, links in the back and download.

I hate to break it to you, but we're all just basic bitches hiding in skin sacks. We can't control these instinctive desires, our brains want them whether we want to be sophisticated or not.

That's cool Sacha, but what the fuck has that got to do with giving the reader what they want?

Well, dear reader, you can give the reader what they want by playing on some of these carnal desires. How many books can you think of with beauty? *Pretties* by Scott Westerfeld or the classic play *Pygmalion* by George Bernard Shaw where Eliza Doolittle gets transformed. The recent Netflix *Bridgerton* series was filled to the brim with wealth and beauty and more often than not, delicious, exquisite meals. And both seasons were complete with competitions to win husbands—competition is another thing we're wired for, survival of the fittest anyone? I'm telling you, we're all basic. As basic as our instincts and rather than fighting it, we should just lean into it.

Besides, don't you just love writing about the things that you secretly desire? Your guilty pleasures? Don't we all really want to be whisked off our feet and loved unconditionally and showered with gifts and an amazing life and romance and joy or whatever else tickles your tinkle?

Apply the same methodology. Examine any sentences that relate to a trope. What do they tell you? What makes them work? Apply to your own work. Rinse and repeat.

3.5 THE ART OF IMPLEMENTATION

There always has to be a last word. This is a final 329 words. Same, same. You made it this far, allow a short additional blathering.

Before I open my mouth, I know you might not want to listen to this. But one of the most common questions I hear when people learn about how I read is, "but what do I do with all the tabs and notes and analysis?"

No one likes the answer.

No one.

But I'll lay it out for you...

You have to put it into practice.

Do the do.

Then take what you've learned and... oh, I dunno... write some fucking words?

It's shocking, I know. Writers spend eighty-five percent of their time weeping, screwing up post-its, voice memoing rants to their friends, drinking gin and staring at screens till their eyeballs bleed red-liquid words.

What do you mean, that's just me?

Liars.

Hate to break it to you chaps, but this is the bit where you have to actually do what this book is telling you. It's horrible, no one ever does the exercises, we all race to the end of the book and conveniently forget all the questions and takeaways we were supposed to be implementing.

BUT DON'T.

GOD DAMMIT.

Of all the craft books you've read, this is the one to implement. If you don't implement it, then you won't change the way you read or be able to deconstruct what other authors are doing. And then where's your best seller at?

You gotta practice, you gotta read like a writer, honeyboo. Analyze what other writers have done and then decide if you like it and use the tools you discover to write an even better book.

It's the *using* of the tools part that'll help you carve out your potential for success.

So go forth, deconstruct like a forensic book worm on steroids.

Sharpen thy word-scalpels, clean your market-glasses, and be one with best sellers.

STEP 3 IMPLEMENT SUMMARY

Where we repeated shit over and over, discovered that practice really does make perfect, and stuck our fingers in the mucky market pie.

- It's not just practice you need, it's *purposeful, focused, intentional* practice.

Consider deconstructing other sources:

- Famous quotes
- Song lyrics
- Poetry
- Short stories and flash fiction
- Film and TV
- Consider sales copy
- Book blurbs
- Newsletter emails
- Short stories and flash fiction

- I shan't be summarizing the implement sections because that would give me a headache. If you want a summary, skip back and reread.

- What is your goal for the book you're writing?
- Readers of each genre want something specific. That does not always connect with what we want to write as authors.

Market layers:

- Layer One: Shit that changes frequently = the books at the top of the charts.
- Layer Two: Shit that changes less frequently = trends, covers, new niches.
- Layer Three: Shit that never changes = the core and heart of a genre.

- Consider analyzing the reviews of your competition's books.
- Follow the charts over time not just one-off checks.
- Watch what comparison authors do on their socials, in their newsletters and advertising wise.
- Don't forget societal impacts on markets and genres.

WANT MORE?

You did it!

We've reached the end, but there's just three more things before you go.

First of all, if you'd like to get a cheat sheet with some more examples of deconstruction, you can get that for free right here: sachablack.co.uk/bestseller

Secondly, I hope you found this book helpful in your quest to understand how your favorite authors are killing it and how you can, too. If you liked the book and can spare a few minutes, I would be really grateful for a short review on the site from which you purchased the book. Reviews are invaluable to an author as it helps us gain visibility and provides the social proof we need to continue selling books. So pretty please with a best seller cherry on top... I will be forever grateful.

Third, if you're looking for a supportive writing community, I run The Rebel Author podcast and community. You can listen to the podcast here: pod.link/rebelauthor

And join the thriving Patreon community where you'll get support, writer chat, lives, writing sprints, movie nights and more. Find out more here: patreon.com/sachablack

ACKNOWLEDGMENTS

Anyone who tells you writing is a solitary exercise is either lying or hasn't found their community yet.

Writing is anything but solitary for me. There are so many people to thank.

First, Cassie. If it weren't for you pushing, nudging and forcefully encouraging me by delivering brilliant covers into my messages, this book wouldn't exist. Your support and enthusiasm literally made this book come to fruition. Thank you because I am really proud of what it became.

To my rebel readers, and specifically those at the masterclass level, thank you for sticking with me, for being so supportive and enthusiastic about the classes and deconstruction. Without your help and willingness to be part of the early classes, I couldn't have figured out how to make what was subconscious, conscious, in order to share it with the wider world. You guys are amazing, patient, supportive, and you give me the warm fuzzies—but don't ask me in public for I'll deny it all. Thank you for sticking with me, I adore you all.

To the rebel patrons and community, honestly, you guys are why I get out of bed every day. Thank you for being so supportive of me and to each other. The community is nothing without you.

To my wife and son. You are my inspiration, my motivation, my purpose. Thank you for everything you do for me.

To Elli, my strengths coach. You are phenomenal, a life changer, a savage butt-kicker, a legit genius. There aren't enough words or thanks that I can write to convey the depths of my gratitude.

To my sprinters: Simone, Kate, Katie and Meg. Thank you for the morning kicks and whip cracks.

And to you, the reader. Without you, there are no books, no markets and no best sellers. Thank you for reading this book, it really does mean the world.

AUTHOR'S NOTE

This book nearly didn't happen. If it weren't for the nudging from Cassie, I'd never have put pen to paper.

Why?

Because this book is more personal, more vulnerable than anything I've ever written. It felt like I was stripping naked in the middle of a class and cutting my soul open to bare all. This book is less, "facts about craft" and more, "this is my personal process". That makes it a lot harder to let go of and publish for so many reasons.

1. It won't work for everyone, and I like to put out books that help as many people as possible.
2. It's painfully personal and I haven't ever really talked about my process in public before.
3. I thought that this process (and the deconstruction work) was something everyone did, so I didn't value it as much as I should have. I had no idea it wasn't universal for writers, and that made it scarier to talk about.

4. Because of the above, the doubt and imposter syndrome were intense.

Weirdly, this is the fastest nonfiction book I've ever written —probably because it was more about a process I do rather than story craft facts. But despite that pace, I had to fight myself the entire way through the marketing and book launch process. I put things off. I avoided sending copies out. It was a lot of mental legwork.

All this is to say, I've written a lot of books and apparently each one can surprise you. Sometimes they're easy and sometimes they're brutal. But the ones that are more personal and closer to your heart are always filled with mental strife.

That said, I think this is one of my best nonfiction books. I'm so proud of having pushed through the fear to actually deliver a finished product.

ABOUT THE AUTHOR

Sacha Black is a bestselling and competition winning author, rebel podcaster, speaker and casual rule breaker. She has five obsessions; words, expensive shoes, conspiracy theories, self-improvement, and breaking the rules. She also has the mind of a perpetual sixteen-year-old, only with slightly less drama and slightly more bills.

Sacha writes books about people with magical powers, sapphic fiction for teens, and other books about the art of writing. She lives in Cambridgeshire, England, with her wife and genius, giant of a son.

When she's not writing, she can be found laughing inappropriately loud, blogging, sniffing musty old books, fangirling film and TV soundtracks, or thinking up new ways to break the rules.

sachablack.co.uk/newsletter
www.sachablack.co.uk
sachablack@sachablack.co.uk

Image Credit @Lastmanphotography

instagram.com/sachablackauthor
bookbub.com/authors/sacha-black
facebook.com/sachablackauthor
twitter.com/sacha_black
amazon.com/author/sachablack

ALSO BY SACHA BLACK

The Better Writers Series

Sacha has a range of books for writers. If you want to improve your villains, your heroes or your prose, she's got you covered.

To improve your villains:

13 Steps to Evil: How to Craft a Superbad Villain
13 Steps to Evil: How to Craft a Superbad Villain Workbook

To improve your heroes:

10 Steps to Hero: How to Craft a Kickass Protagonist
10 Steps To Hero - How To Craft A Kickass Protagonist Workbook

To improve your side characters:

8 Steps to Side Characters: How to Craft Supporting Roles with Intention, Purpose, and Power
8 Steps to Side Characters: How to Craft Supporting Roles with Intention, Purpose, and Power Workbook

To improve your prose:

The Anatomy of Prose: 12 Steps to Sensational Sentences

The Anatomy of Prose: 12 Steps to Sensational Sentences Workbook

RESOURCES

Malcolm Gladwell, YouTube Link: https://www.youtube.-com/watch?v=1uB5PUpGzeY

Printed in Great Britain
by Amazon

14523457R00129